Learning to Read Using Phonics

BOOK 1

Author
Mara Ellen Guckian

Editor in Chief
Brent L. Fox, M. Ed.

Creative Director
Sarah M. Fournier

Cover Artist
Diem Pascarella

Illustrator
Kevin Cameron

Art Coordinator
Renée Mc Elwee

Imaging
Amanda R. Harter

Publisher
Mary D. Smith, M.S. Ed.

Teacher Created Resources
12621 Western Avenue
Garden Grove, CA 92841
www.teachercreated.com
ISBN: 978-1-4206-1707-8
©2022 Teacher Created Resources
Reprinted, 2025

Made in U.S.A.

For standards correlations, visit
http://www.teachercreated.com/standards/.

Teacher Created Resources

Table of Contents

Introduction

Learning to Read Using Phonics was developed to help young learners practice sounding out words as they begin learning to read. This book focuses on the relationship between the sounds and letters that represent the English language. There are 26 letters in the English language. These letters represent 44 different sounds!

Words can be segmented (broken up) into individual *phonemes*—the smallest unit of spoken language. For example, the word *bat* has three phonemes or sounds: /b/ /a/ /t/. Being able to *blend* sounds into words is a very important component when learning to read fluently and spell correctly.

Young learners are encouraged to sound out words based on the pictures they see and to convert the sounds they hear to letters of the alphabet. This ability to isolate sounds is known as *phonemic awareness*.

Learners also practice writing by tracing using developmentally appropriate lines and letter patterns. The goal is to continue to reinforce the correct formation of each letter and to introduce correct spacing between words and ending punctuation marks. An added bonus is that as they practice, they are developing word recognition skills and learning to spell new words!

Getting Started

Review the 100 Sight Words, Direction Words, and Color Words lists on pages 5–7. These reference lists represent important words young learners will frequently see as they begin their "learning to read" journey.

First 100 Sight Words—The words on page 5 are also known as "high frequency words." Sight words are the most common words readers will come across. They are usually the first words students are asked to learn at school. Many of these words do not follow regular spelling patterns and must be memorized.

Point out these words when reading to children to increase awareness of them. Soon, your young learners will be pointing out the words to you in books, on signs, and other written materials.

Direction Words—At first, you will need to read the directions and explain how to complete each page in the book. As you share the directions, emphasize reading from left to right and note that there are spaces between words. Point out the "direction" words. It may be helpful to show them page 6, so that they can equate a picture symbol with the direction word.

Color Words—As young learners master the sounds of the alphabet, they can begin to sound out words. Reinforce the color words on page 7 by having them trace each word in the appropriate color.

Share these lists when appropriate, either as references or for frequent reviews with children.

Hopefully, you and your young learners will enjoy exploring sounds, building words, and reading together.

How to Use This Book

The different sections of this book follow a natural progression to help young readers and writers develop a solid foundation. The activities are presented to allow young learners to identify sounds, then letters. From there, they can proceed to reading (decoding) and writing (encoding) words and combining words to make sentences:

- First, young learners focus on the most common sound attributed to each alphabet letter, Aa–Zz. Tracing lines are provided to help develop proper printing skills.

- Beginning and ending consonant sounds are examined next, followed by short vowel sounds. Young learners will continue to identify items through pictures and naming items, and will focus on the beginning, middle, or ending sounds they hear. Practice is provided for short vowel rhyming words, word families, and reading sentences.

- Next, readers will explore long vowels, more rhyming word practice, and long vowel word families. Sentences with long vowel words are included.

- The final section introduces young learners to two-letter blends. In these blends, each letter of the blend is pronounced quickly, so they "blend together." (_flower, sleep, glass_) You can hear both letters, but the sounds go together smoothly.

- Use the Answer Key (pages 110–112) as a guide to what each picture could represent. The goal, in phonics, is to identify the correct sound in order to determine the correct letter. Ask what the picture is before saying it is incorrect. It might not be. If, for instance, your child sees a picture of a _dog_ on a "d" page, and says it begins with a "p" because it is a _puppy_, that is ok. Their answer depends upon the sound they hear. You might then ask, "What would it begin with if it was a _dog_?"

Here are some things to practice regularly with young learners:

- Point to an item or a picture. Ask, "What is this?" After naming the item, work together to sound out the letter sounds in the word. /d/ /o/ /g/

- Match sounds to letters.

- Isolate and identify the first, last, and middle sounds heard in words.

dog

- Blend sounds together to make words. _Example:_ Ask, "What word is this?" as you pronounce the proper letter sounds. /b/ /u/ /g/ (_bug_). It should sound like this—"buh" "uh" "guh."

Once young learners are comfortable sounding out and blending, try the following activities:

- Segment words to identify word parts. _Examples:_ Clap word parts for the word _cat_ (c-a-t). Or, ask, "How many sounds do you hear in the word _lime_?" There are three different sounds since the e is silent. /l/ /ī/ /m/

- Delete letters. _Examples:_ Ask a child what word they hear if they take the /m/ sound off the word _farm_, or say _cat_ without the c (_at_).

- Substitute letters (sounds). _Examples:_ Switch beginning sounds to make new rhyming words (_cat, bat, hat_).

- Categorize. _Examples:_ Ask, "Which word does not have the same beginning, middle, or ending sound?" _bug, ball, big, pot, bee_ (_pot_ does not begin with a _b_.)

100 Sight Words List

○ the
○ of
○ and
○ a
○ to
○ in
○ is
○ you
○ that
○ it
○ he
○ was
○ for
○ on
○ are
○ as
○ with
○ his
○ they
○ I
○ at
○ be
○ this
○ have
○ from

○ or
○ one
○ had
○ by
○ words
○ but
○ not
○ what
○ all
○ were
○ we
○ when
○ your
○ can
○ said
○ there
○ use
○ an
○ each
○ which
○ she
○ do
○ how
○ their
○ if

○ will
○ up
○ other
○ about
○ out
○ many
○ then
○ them
○ these
○ so
○ some
○ her
○ would
○ make
○ like
○ him
○ into
○ time
○ has
○ look
○ two
○ more
○ write
○ go
○ see

○ number
○ no
○ way
○ could
○ people
○ my
○ than
○ first
○ water
○ been
○ called
○ who
○ am
○ its
○ now
○ find
○ long
○ down
○ day
○ did
○ get
○ come
○ made
○ may
○ part

Name: _______________________

Direction Words

Directions: Read and trace the direction words. Use the pictures as clues.

Listen

Color

Read

Circle

Group

Find

Trace

Cross

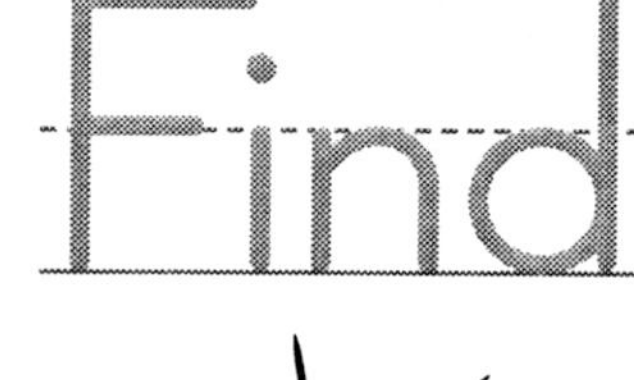

Clap

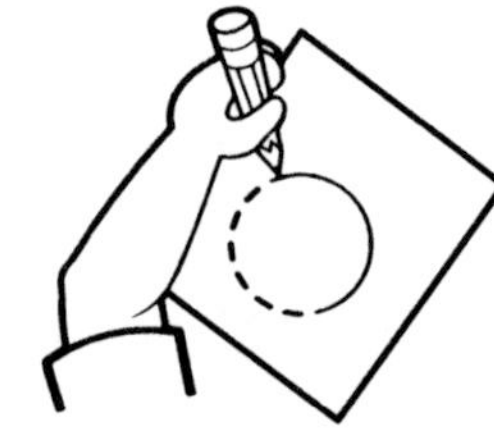

Underline

Write

Name: _______________________

Color Words

Directions: Read the color word in each crayon. Trace the color words using the correct color for each.

red

yellow

green

purple

blue

orange

pink

white

black

gray

tan

brown

Name: _______________________

Sounds Like—Aa, Bb, Cc

Directions: Listen to the beginning sound of each item. Trace and write the letters for each sound.

apple	A A a a
butterfly	B B b b
cat	C C c c

Name: _______________________

Sounds Like—Dd, Ee, Ff

Directions: Listen to the beginning sound of each item. Trace and write the letters for each sound.

dog	D D _____________ d d _____________
elephant	E E _____________ e e _____________
fish	F F _____________ f f _____________

Name: _______________________

Sounds Like—Gg, Hh, Ii

Directions: Listen to the beginning sound of each item. Trace and write the letters for each sound.

goat	G G g g
horse	H H h h
ice	I I i i

Name: _________________________________

Sounds Like—Jj, Kk, Ll

Directions: Listen to the beginning sound of each item. Trace and write the letters for each sound.

jacket	J J J j j j
kangaroo	K K k k
lion	L L l l

Name: ___________________________

Sounds Like—Mm, Nn, Oo

Directions: Listen to the beginning sound of each item. Trace and write the letters for each sound.

mouse	M M m m
nest	N N n n
octopus	O O o o

Name: ________________

Sounds Like—Pp, Qq, Rr

Directions: Listen to the beginning sound of each item. Trace and write the letters for each sound.

peas

P P

p p

quilt

Q Q

q q

ring

R R

r r

Name: _______________________

Sounds Like—Ss, Tt, Uu

Directions: Listen to the beginning sound of each item. Trace and write the letters for each sound.

sun	S S s s
turtle	T T t t
umbrella	U U u u

Name: _______________________________

Sounds Like—Vv, Ww, Xx

Directions: Listen to the beginning sound of each item. Trace and write the letters for each sound.

violin	V V
wagon	W W
x-ray	X X

Name: _______________________

Sounds Like—Yy, Zz

Directions: Listen to the beginning sound of each item. Trace and write the letters for each sound.

yo-yo

zebra

Directions: Write your name.

Alphabet Fill In

Directions: Write and trace the uppercase or lowercase letters to finish the alphabet chart.

A b c D E

f G H i j

K L M n

o p Q r S

t U v W

x y Z

Name: _______________________

Begins with Bb

Directions: Circle the items that begin with the **b sound**. Cross out the other items.

Directions: Read and trace the sentence. Color the balloon blue.

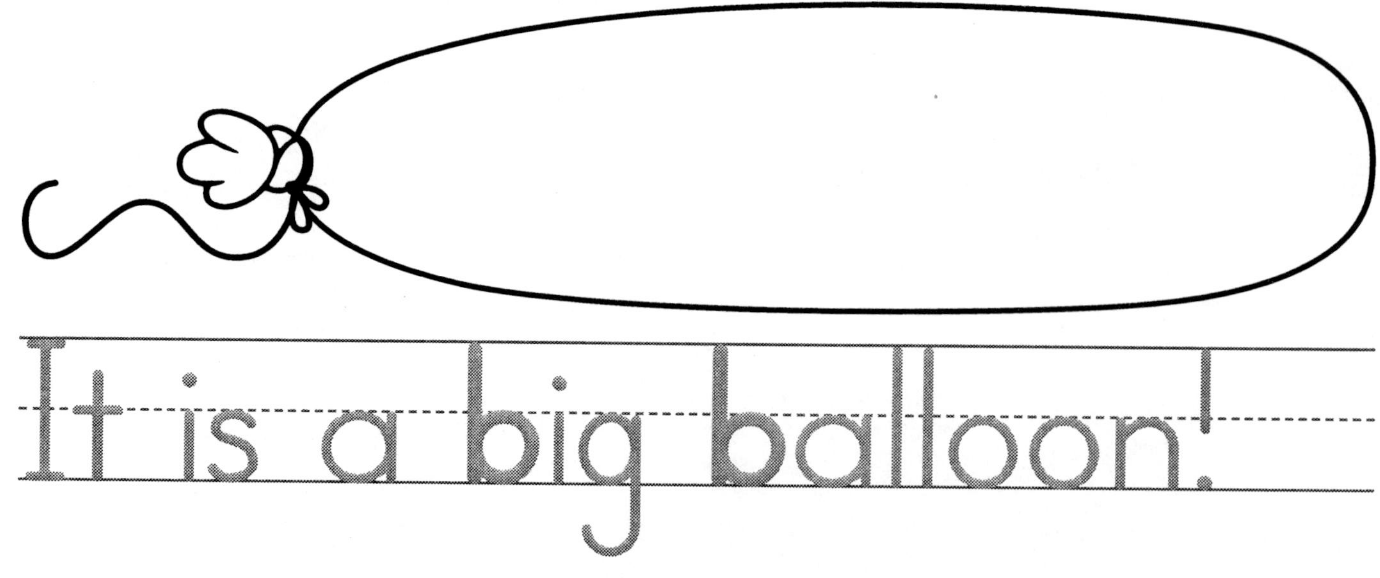

Name: _______________________________

Begins with Cc

Directions: Circle the items that begin with the **c sound**. Cross out the other items.

Directions: Read and trace the sentence. Color the cat orange. Color the car purple.

Name: _______________________________

Begins with Dd

Directions: Circle the items that begin with the **d sound**. Cross out the other items.

Directions: Read and trace the sentence. Color the dog brown.

Name: _______________________

Begins with Ff

Directions: Circle the items that begin with the **f sound**. Cross out the other items.

Directions: Read and trace the sentence. Color the flowers purple and red.

Name: _______________________

Bb, Cc, Dd, or Ff?

Directions: Listen to the beginning sound of each item. Write the beginning letter and trace the other letters to complete each word. Read each word.

at	og	an
at	rum	an
oot	ox	ell

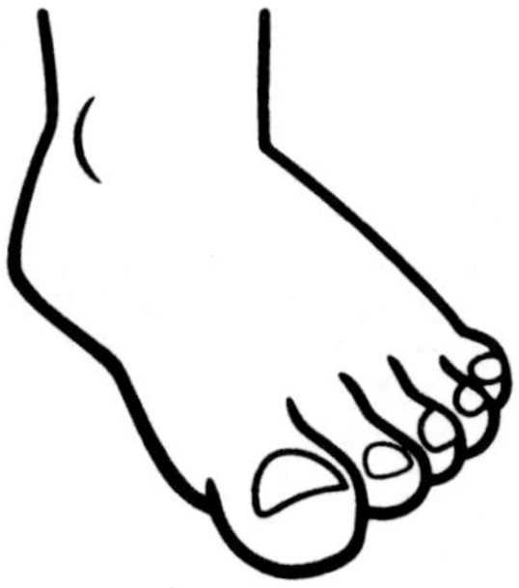

Name: _______________________

Begins with Gg

Directions: Circle the items that begin with the **g sound**. Cross out the other items.

Directions: Read and trace the sentence. Color the girl and the geese.

Name: _______________________

Begins with Hh

Directions: Circle the items that begin with the **h sound**. Cross out the other items.

Directions: Read and trace the sentence. Color the horse gray.

Name: _______________________________

Begins with Jj

Directions: Circle the items that begin with the **j sound**. Cross out the other items.

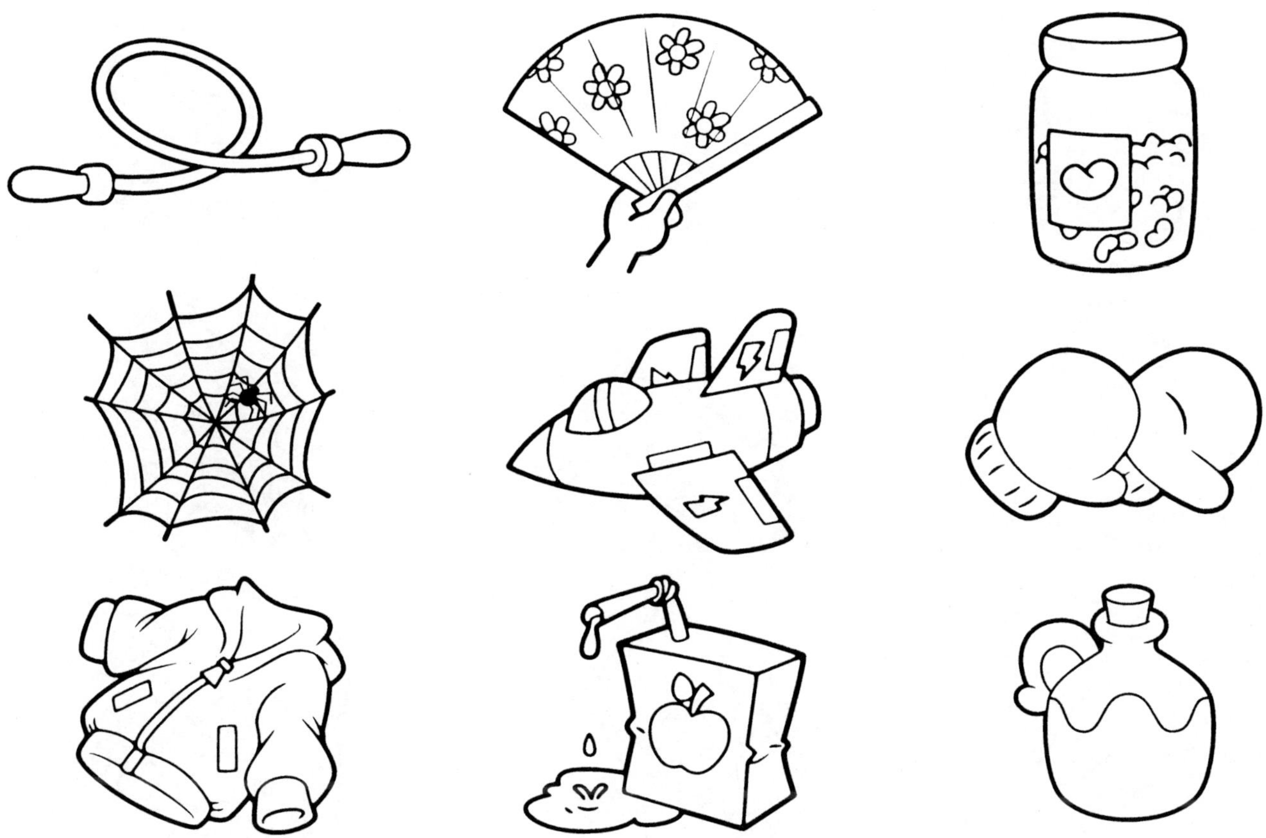

Directions: Read and trace the sentence. Color the jam purple.

He has a jar of jam.

Name: _______________________

Begins with Kk

Directions: Circle the items that begin with the **k sound**. Cross out the other items.

Directions: Read and trace the sentence. Color the koala gray.

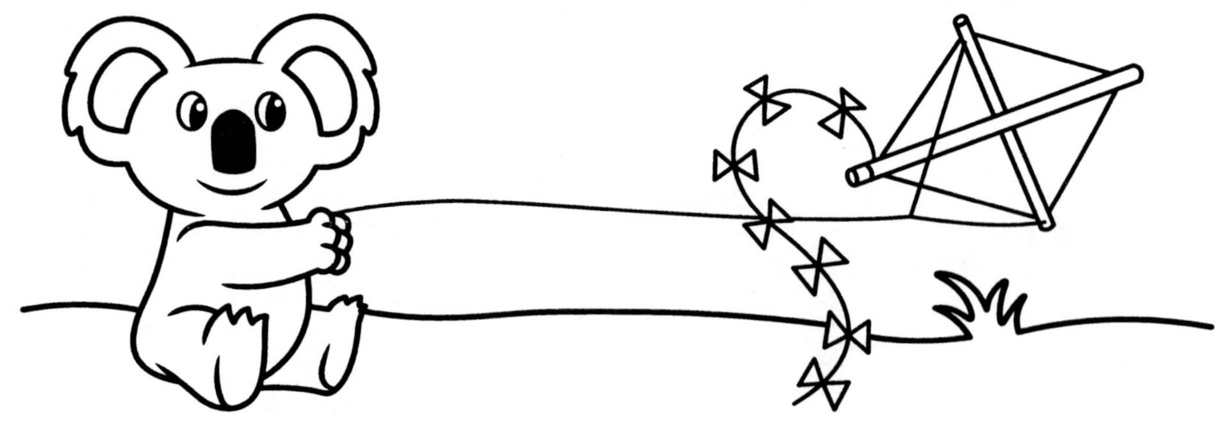

The koala has a kite.

Name: _______________________

Gg, Hh, Jj, or Kk?

Directions: Listen to the beginning sound of each item. Write the beginning letter and trace the other letters to complete each word. Read each word.

___ive	___et	___ate
___ar	___ose	___ing
___as	___ite	___and

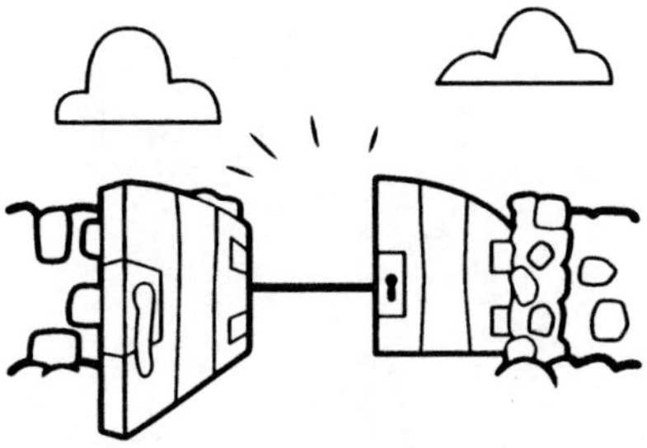

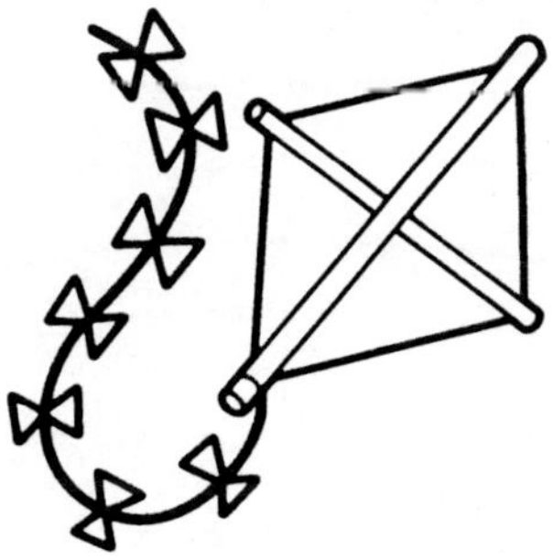

Name: ___________________________

Begins with Ll

Directions: Circle the items that begin with the **l sound**. Cross out the other items.

Directions: Read and trace the sentence. Color the lizard green and the log brown.

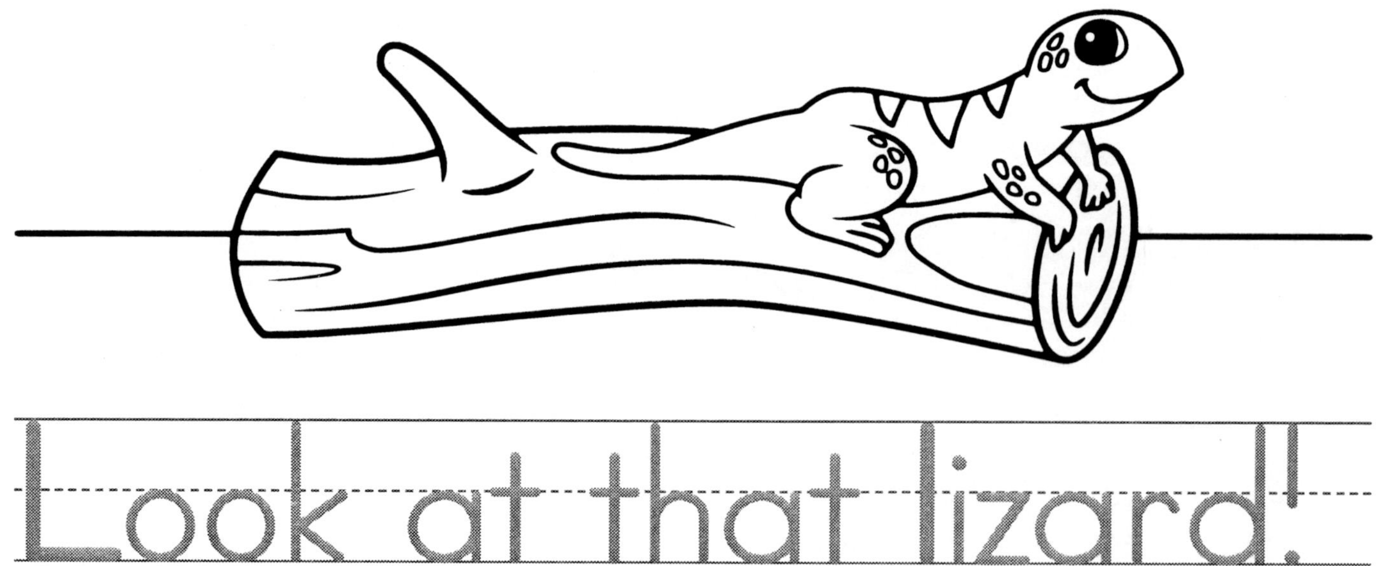

Name: _______________________

Begins with Mm

Directions: Circle the items that begin with the **m sound**. Cross out the other items.

Directions: Read and trace the sentence. Color the monkey brown.

Name: _______________________

Begins with Nn

Directions: Circle the items that begin with the **n sound**. Cross out the other items.

Directions: Read and trace the sentence. Color the nuts tan and the squirrel gray.

Name: _______________________________

Begins with Pp

Directions: Circle the items that begin with the **p sound**. Cross out the other items.

Directions: Read and trace the sentence. Color the pig pink and the mud brown.

A pig plays in a pen.

Name: _______________________________

Ll, Mm, Nn, or Pp?

Directions: Listen to the beginning sound of each item. Write the beginning letter and trace the other letters to complete each word. Read each word.

___en	___eg	___oon
___ug	___an	___et
___est	___amp	___ot

Name: _______________________________

Begins with Qq

Directions: Circle the items that begin with the **q sound**. Cross out the other items.

Directions: Read and trace the sentence. Color the quilt different colors. Color the quail black and brown.

Name: _______________________

Begins with Rr

Directions: Circle the items that begin with the **r sound**. Cross out the other items.

Directions: Read and trace the sentence. Color the rug blue and the ram brown.

Name: _______________________

Begins with Ss

Directions: Circle the items that begin with the **s sound**. Cross out the other items.

Directions: Read and trace the sentence. Color the stars yellow. Count the stars.

We saw seven stars.

Name: _______________________

Begins with Tt

Directions: Circle the items that begin with the **t sound**. Cross out the other items.

Directions: Read and trace the sentence. Color the toy truck orange.

Name: _______________________

Qq, Rr, Ss, or Tt?

Directions: Listen to the beginning sound of each item. Write the beginning letter and trace the other letters to complete each word. Read each word.

__uilt	__en	__un
__ake	__ing	__ock
__op	__ix	__uail

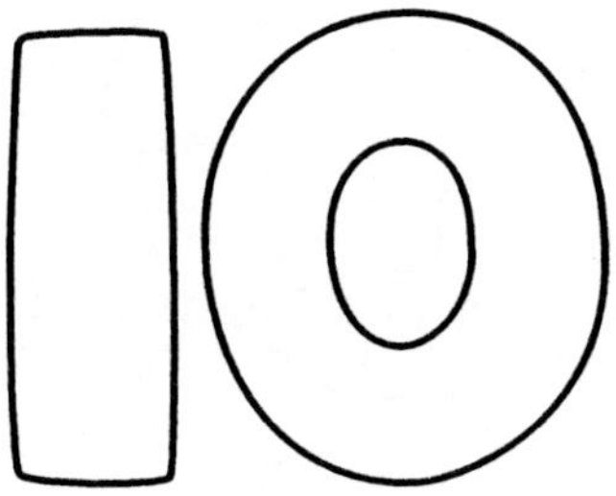

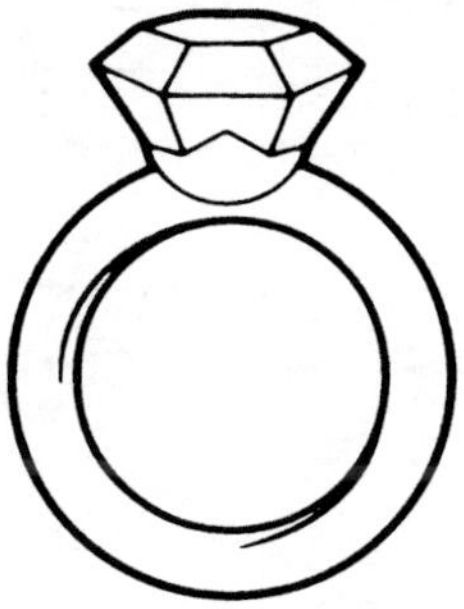

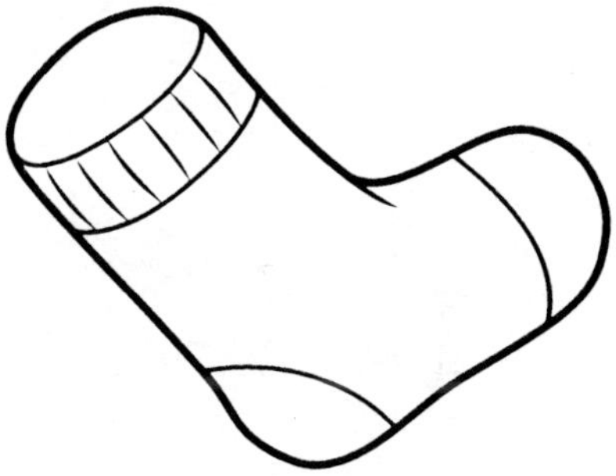

Name: ___________________

Begins with Vv

Directions: Circle the items that begin with the **v sound**. Cross out the other items.

Directions: Read and trace the sentence. Color the vase pink and the flowers yellow.

It is a very big vase.

Name: _______________________________

Begins with Ww

Directions: Circle the items that begin with the **w sound**. Cross out the other items.

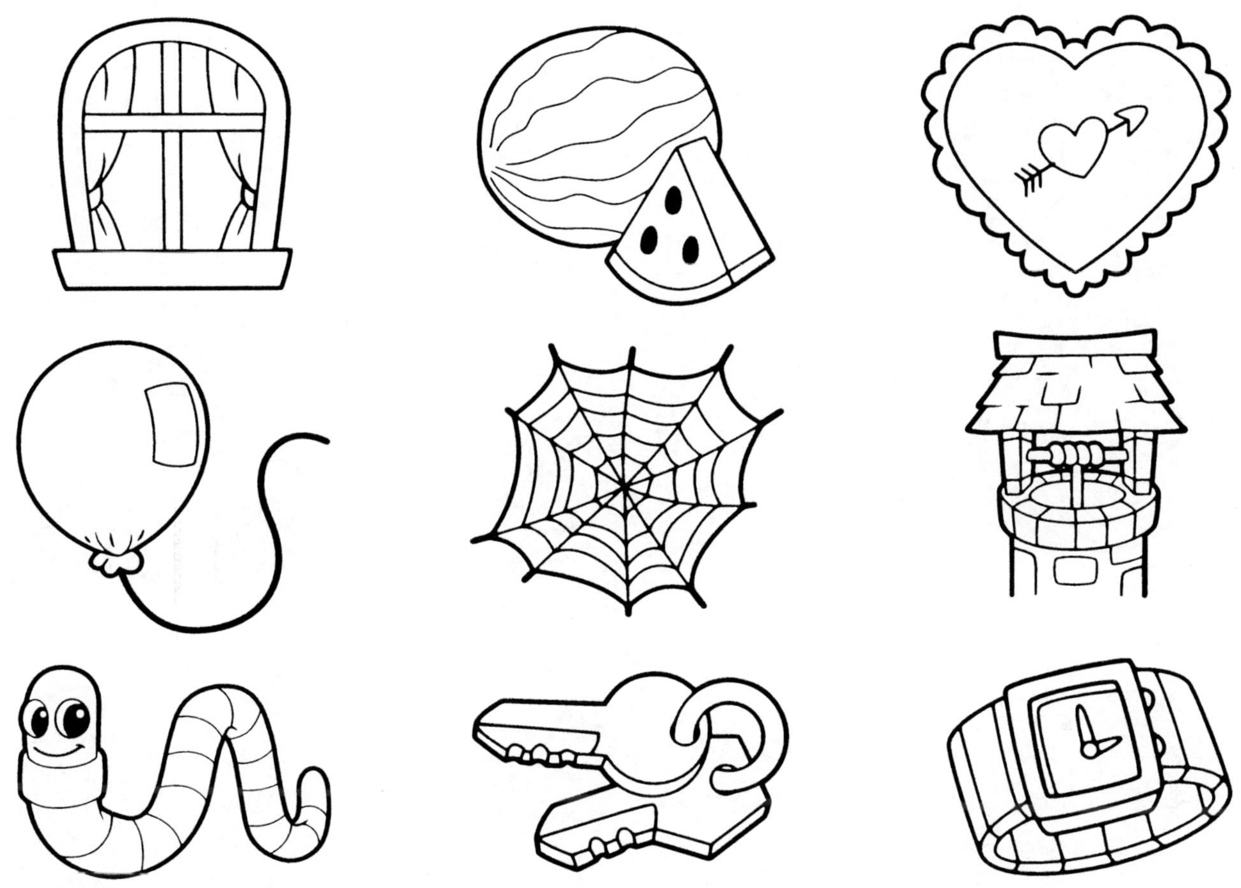

Directions: Read and trace the sentence. Color the wall red and the walrus brown.

Name: ______________________________

Begins with Yy

Directions: Circle the items that begin with the **y sound**. Cross out the other items.

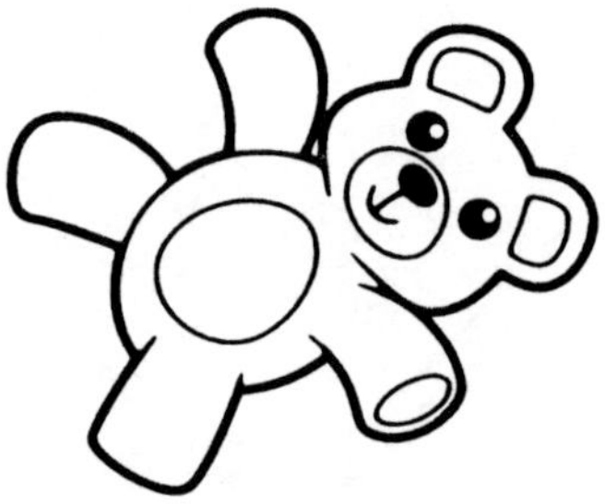

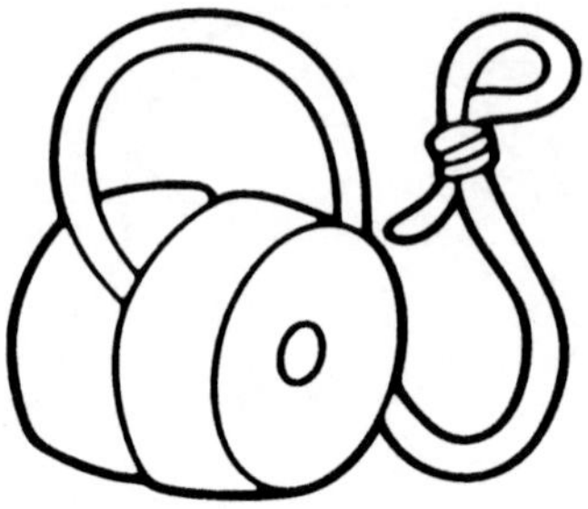

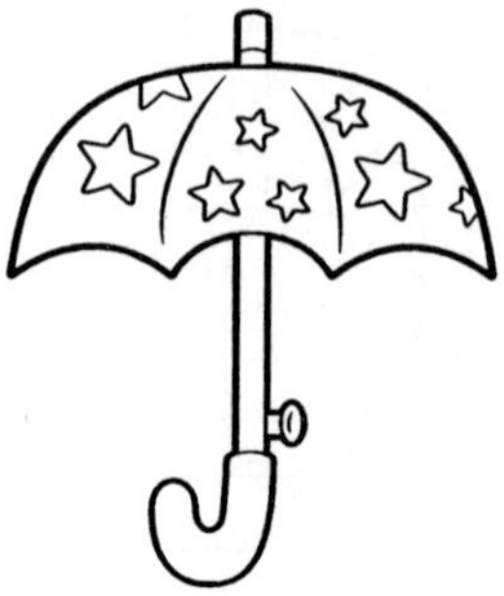

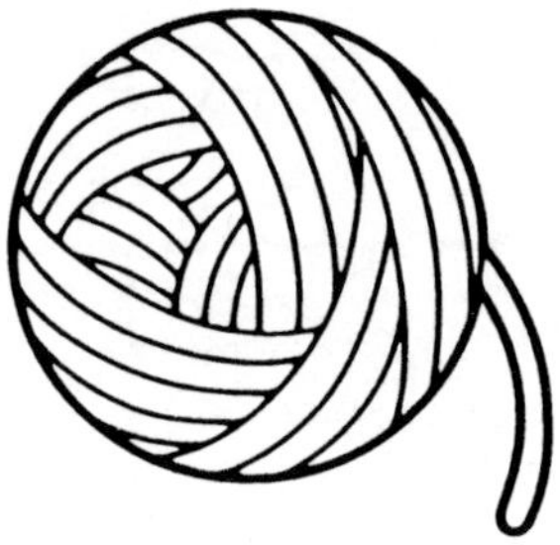

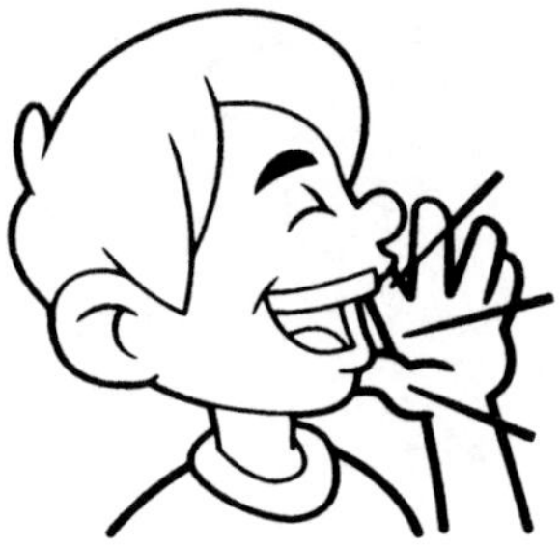

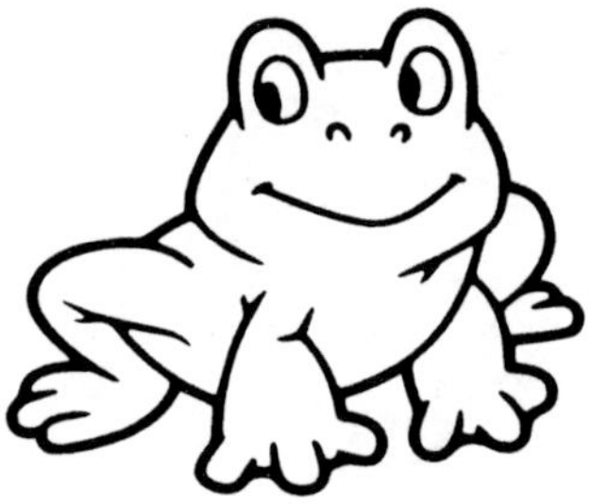

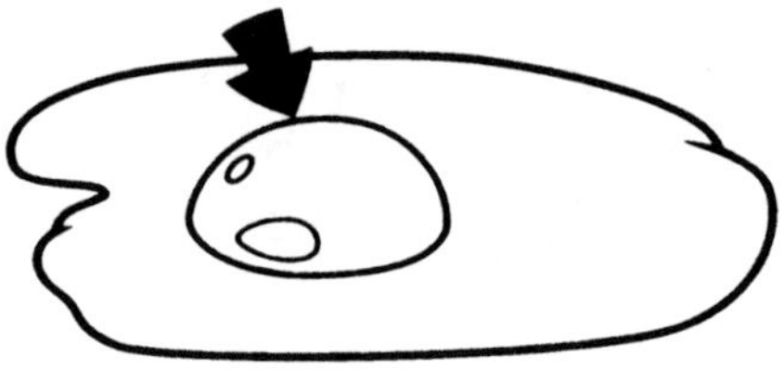

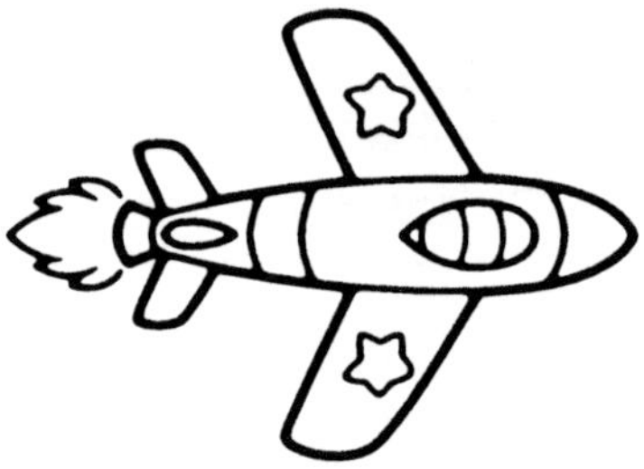

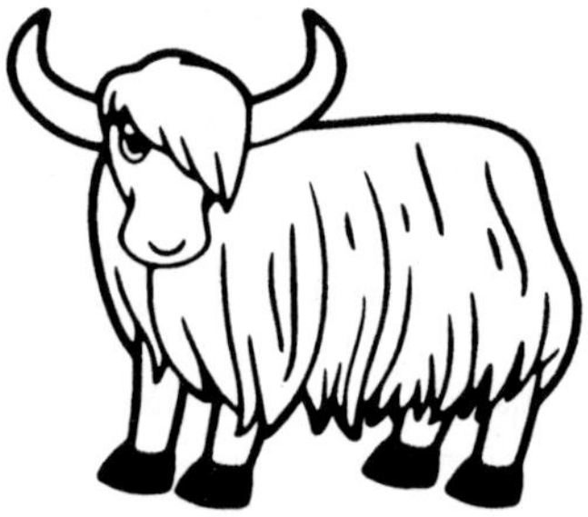

Directions: Read and trace the sentence. Color the yo-yo yellow.

This yo-yo is yellow.

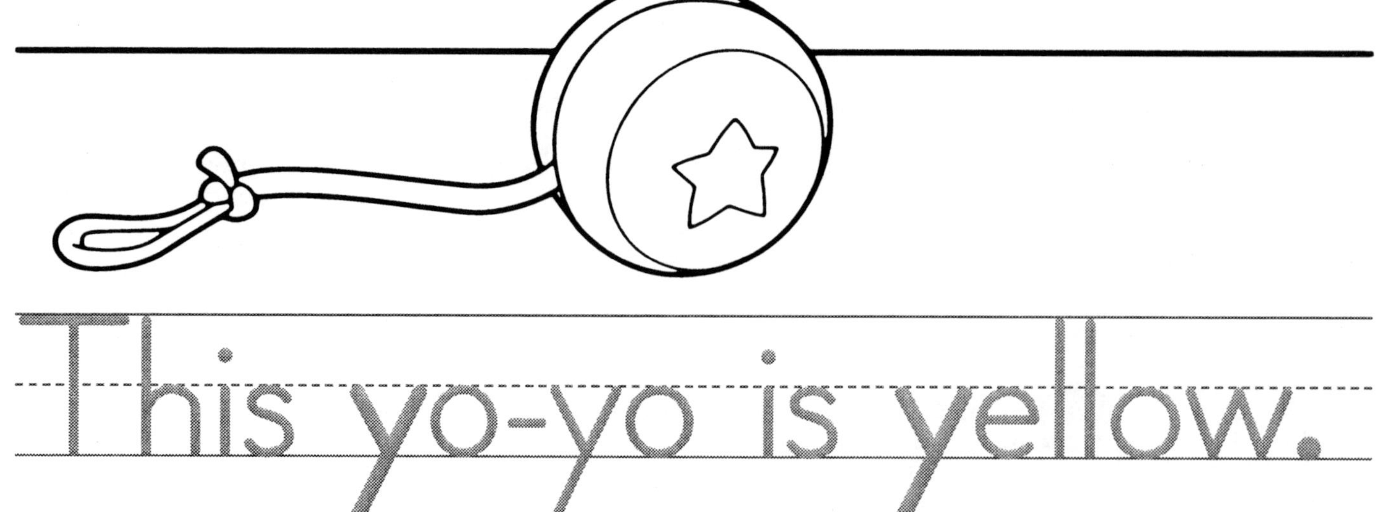

Name: _______________________________

Begins with Zz

Directions: Circle the items that begin with the **z sound**. Cross out the other items.

Directions: Read and trace the sentence. Color the grass green and the mountains brown.

Name: _______________________

Vv, Ww, Yy, or Zz?

Directions: Listen to the beginning sound of each item. Write the beginning letter and trace the other letters to complete each word. Read each word.

ipper	iolin	o-yo
atch	agon	ase
ebra	arn	orm

Name: _______________________

Choose the Beginning Sound

Directions: Fill in the circle that has the letter for the beginning sound for each animal.

h f p b	s h l c	g d b h
k g t r	m w s n	m n w y
g j p q	c v s x	q p y j

Name: _______________________

More Beginning Sounds

Directions: Fill in the circle that has the letter for the beginning sound for each animal.

d p b q	g j p y	r z m n
h t k l	s c n r	c b z r
j y f h	b d f h	n w l t

Which Is It?

Directions: Listen to the beginning sound of each item. Fill the circle with the letter for that beginning sound.

©Teacher Created Resources

#9101 *Learning to Read Using Phonics*

Name: _______________________

Ends with Bb

Directions: Circle the items that end with the **b sound**. Cross out the other item.

Directions: Add a **b** to the end of each word. Trace and read the word.

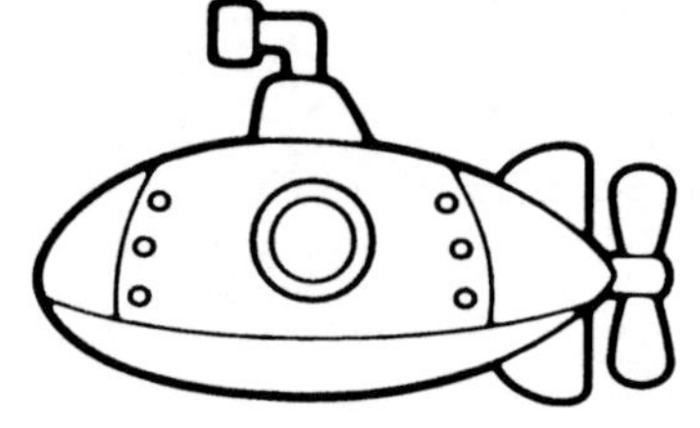  

su____   cu____   bi____

Directions: Read and trace the sentence. <u>Underline</u> the words that end in **b**.

Bob put a sub in
the big tub.

Name: _______________________________

Ends with Dd

Directions: Circle the items that end with the **d sound**. Cross out the items that have a different ending sound.

Directions: Trace and read the sight words. Write the words two more times. <u>Underline</u> the ending letter **d**.

and

had

Directions: Draw a face for each word that ends in **d**.

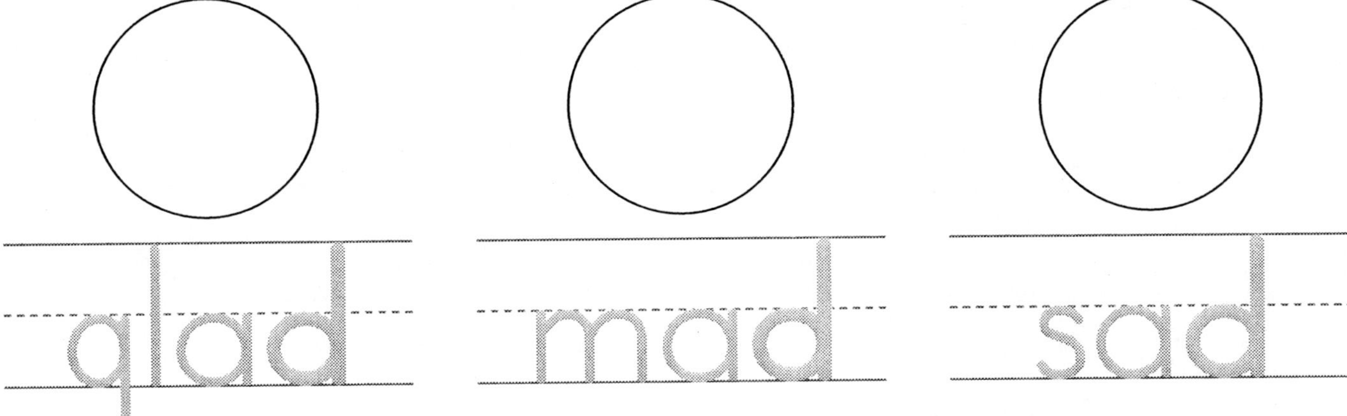

glad   mad   sad

Name: _______________________________

Ends with Gg

Directions: Circle the items that end with the **g sound**. Cross out the other item.

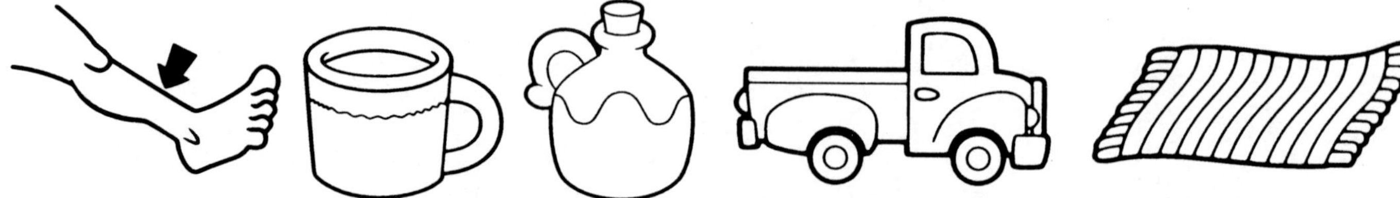

Directions: Write the words that end in **g** for each picture. Which words rhyme?

Directions: Draw a big bug on the log and trace the sentence. <u>Underline</u> the words that end in **g**.

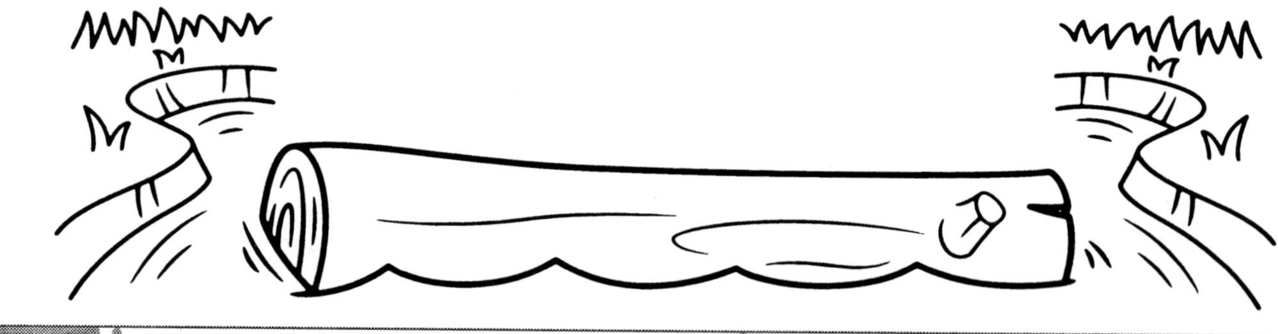

Name: _______________________________

Ends with Ll

Directions: Circle the items that end with the **l sound**. Cross out the other item.

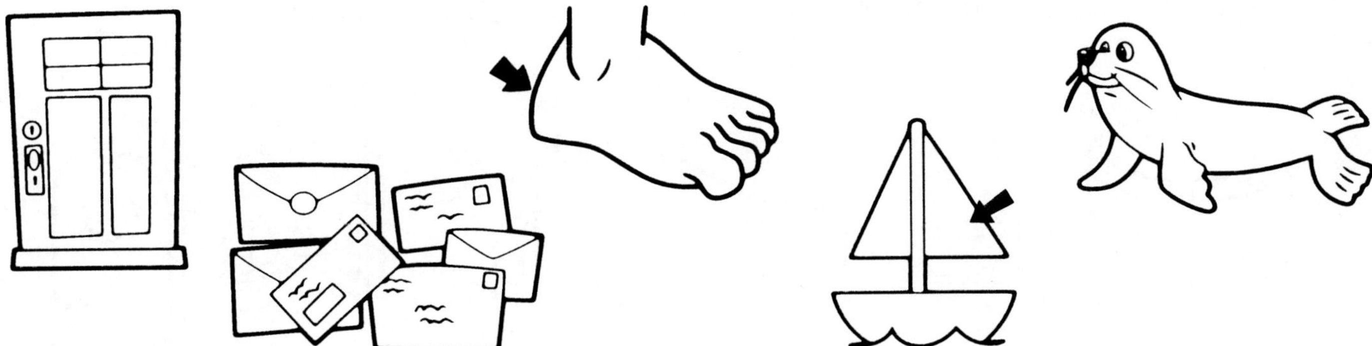

Directions: Trace and read the sight word. Write the word **all** two more times. Circle the ending letters.

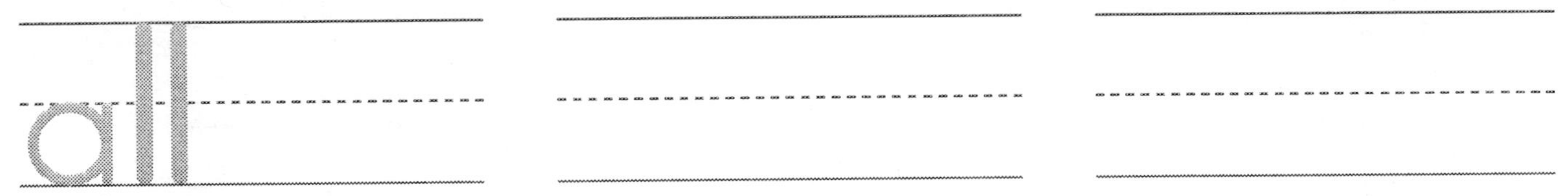

all

Directions: Read and trace the sentence. <u>Underline</u> all the words that end in **l**. Color the hill green.

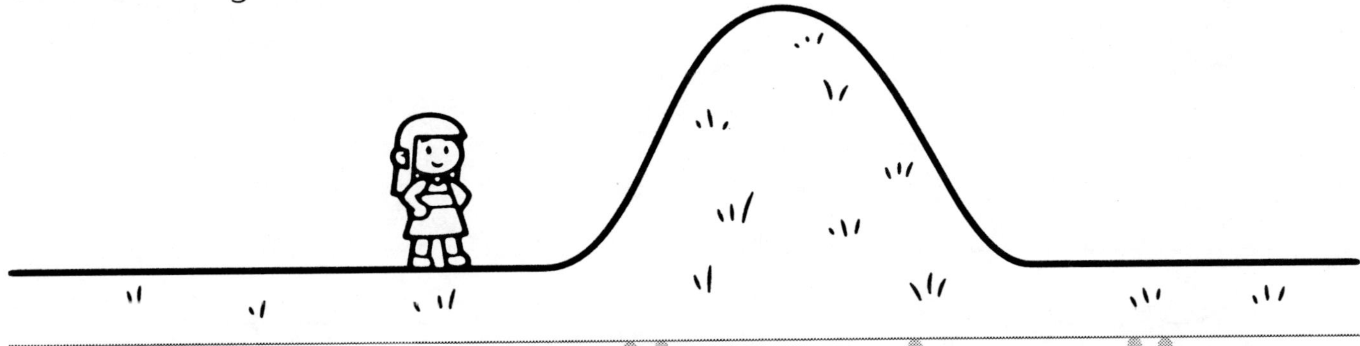

The small girl will

go up the big hill.

Name: _______________________

Bb, Dd, Gg, or Ll?

Directions: Listen to the ending sound for each item. Write the ending letter to complete each word. Trace the other letters and read the words.

mu___

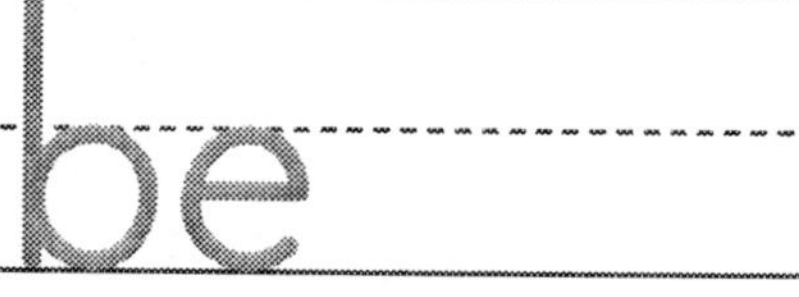

be___

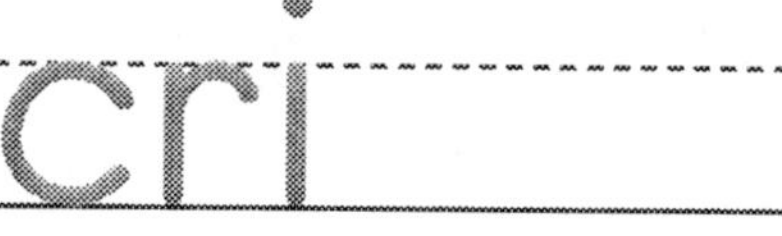

cri___

cu___

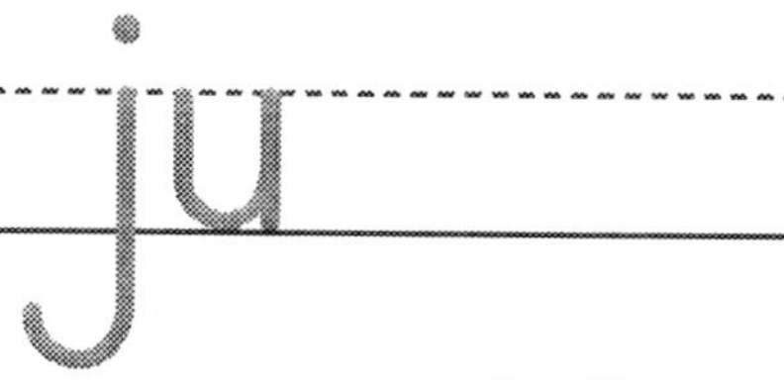

ju___

sea___

we___

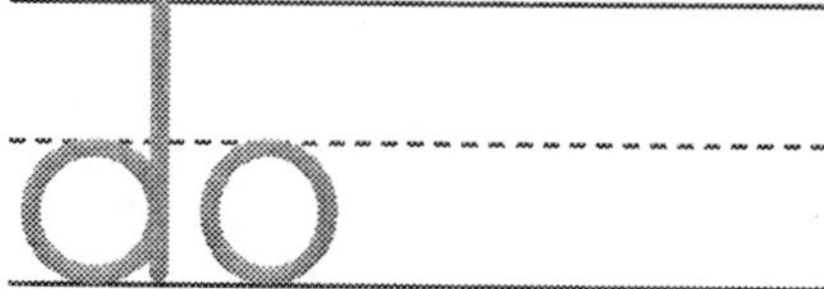

do___

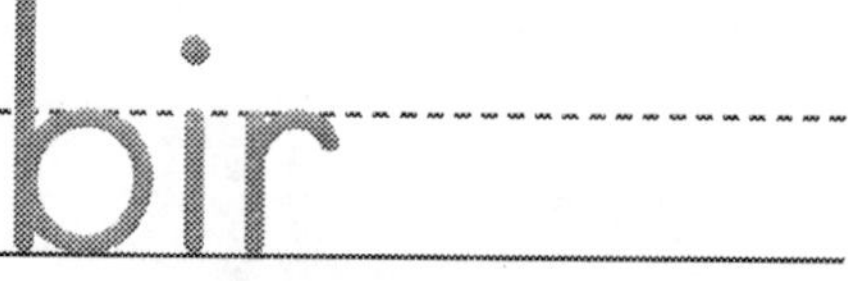

bir___

Name: _______________________

Ends with Mm

Directions: Add an **m** to each group of letters. Then, read the word and draw a line to its picture.

gu___

ha___

ja___

ra___

Directions: Read and trace the sentence. <u>Underline</u> the words that end in **m**.

The ram ran to him.

Name: _______________________

Ends with Nn

Directions: Circle the items that end with the **n sound**. Cross out the others.

Directions: Add an **n** to the end of each group of letters. Read and trace the words. What is different about the words? What is the same?

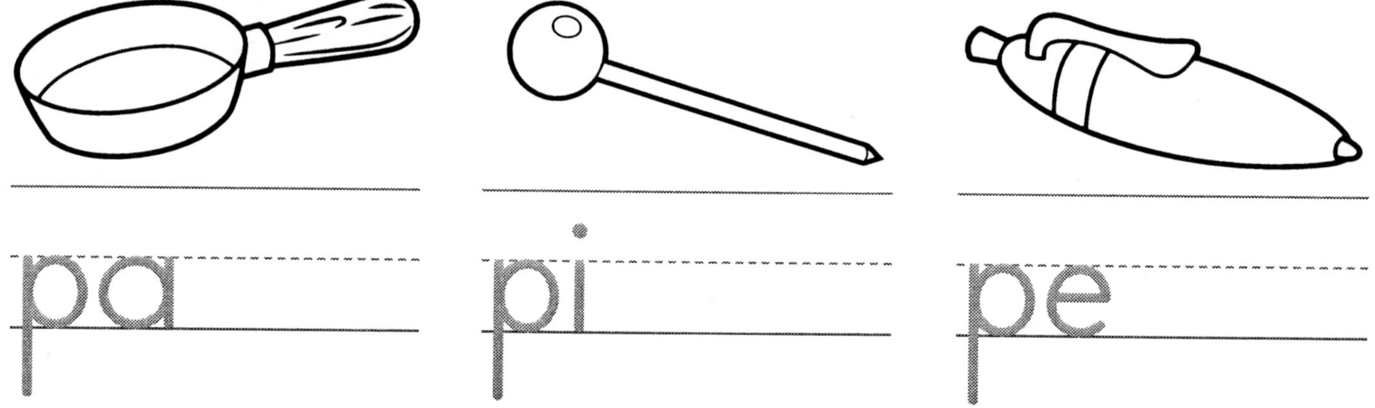

pa______   pi______   pe______

Directions: Read and trace the sentence. <u>Underline</u> the words that end in **n**.

A hen is by the barn.

Name: _______________________________

Ends with Pp

Directions: Circle the items that end with the **p sound**. Cross out the other items.

  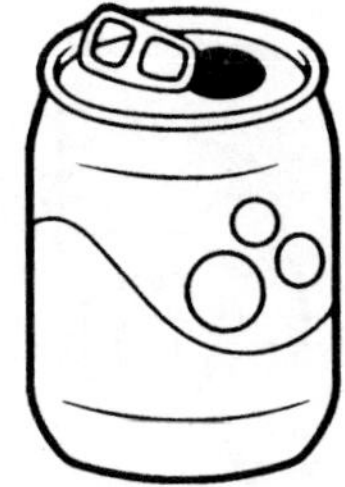

Directions: Read and trace the words below that end in the letter **p**.

 rip 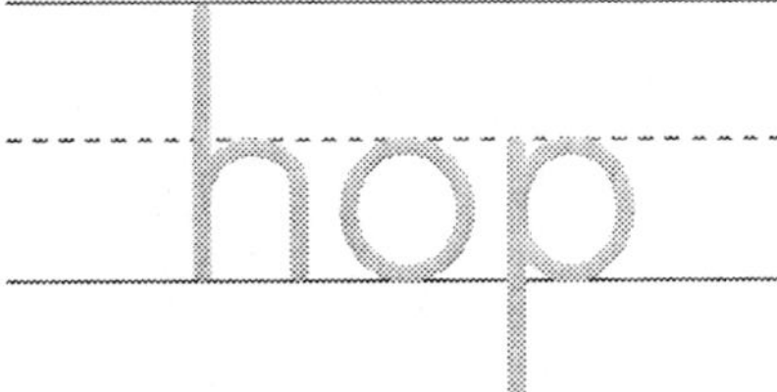 hop 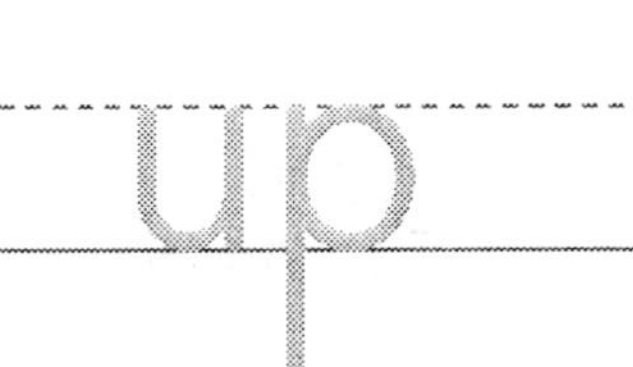 up

Directions: Read and trace the sentence. <u>Underline</u> the words that end in **p**. Color the pup brown.

  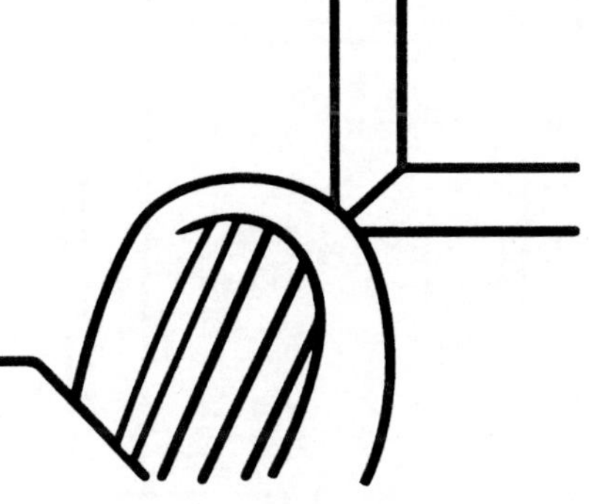

A pup is in a cup.

Name: _______________________

Ends with Rr

Directions: Circle the items that end with the **r sound**. Cross out the other item.

Directions: **Feather** is a two-syllable word that ends in **r**. Count and clap the syllables—*feath-er*. Use a blue crayon to trace the word *feather*.

feather

Directions: Read and trace the sentence. <u>Underline</u> the words that end in **r**. Color the star yellow. Color the doors different colors.

A star is on a door.

Name: _______________________

Mm, Nn, Pp, or Rr?

Directions: Listen to the ending sound for each item. Write the ending letter to complete each word. Trace the other letters and read the words.

cu_

ca_

fa_

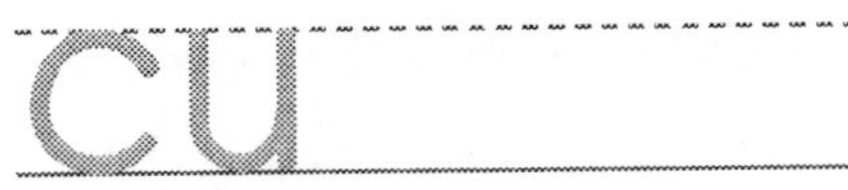

ra_

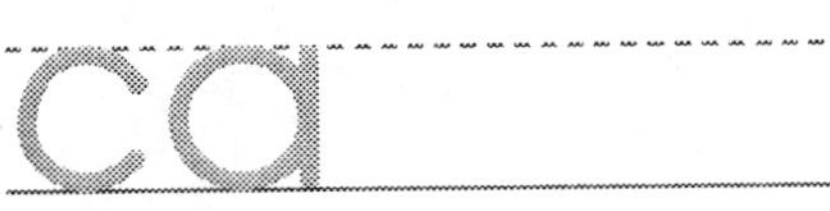

mo_

ja_

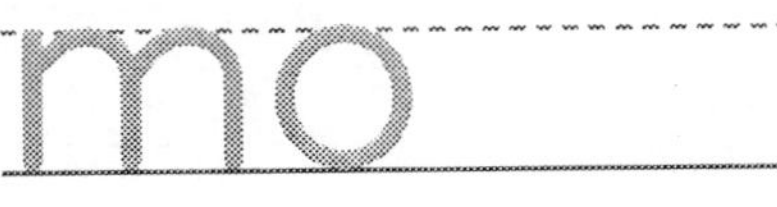

su_

gu_

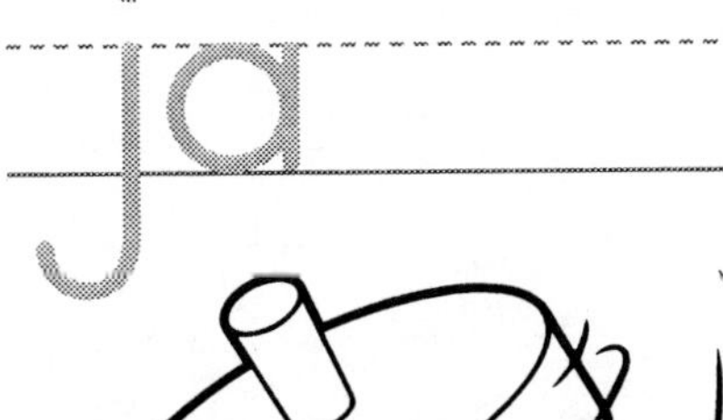

to_

Name: _______________________

Ends with Ss

Directions: Circle the items that end with the **s sound**. Cross out the other items.

Directions: Read and trace each sight word that ends with the **s** sound. Write the letters of each sight word in the boxes.

as

is

has

its

his

was

Name: _______________________________

Ends with Tt

Directions: Add a **t** to each group of letters. Then, read the word and draw a line to its picture.

ha____

ne____

ba____

je____

co____

Directions: **Carrot** is a two-syllable word that ends in **t**. Count and clap the syllables—*car-rot*. Color the carrot orange and green.

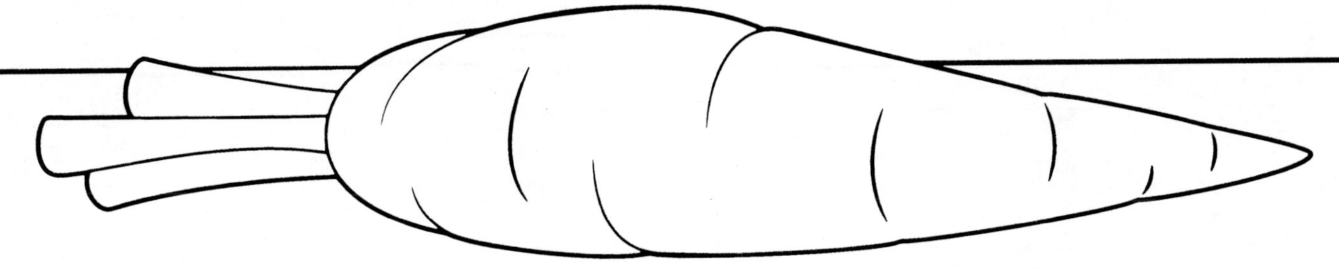

Name: _______________________

Ends with Ww

Directions: Circle the items that end with a **w**. Cross out the other item. The letter **w** is silent at the *end* of the word. It works with the vowel that comes before it.

Directions: Add a **w** to the end of each word and trace each word.

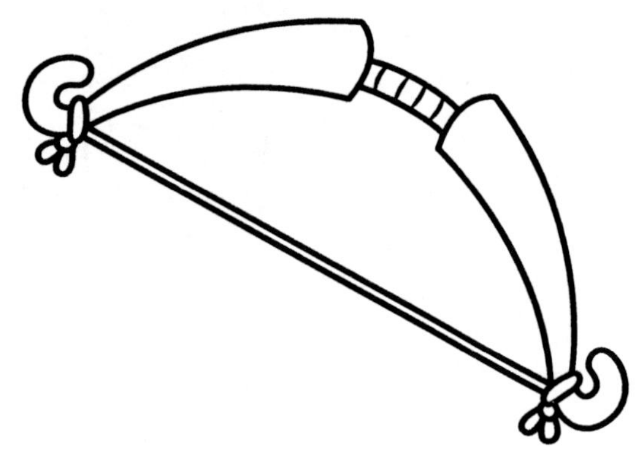 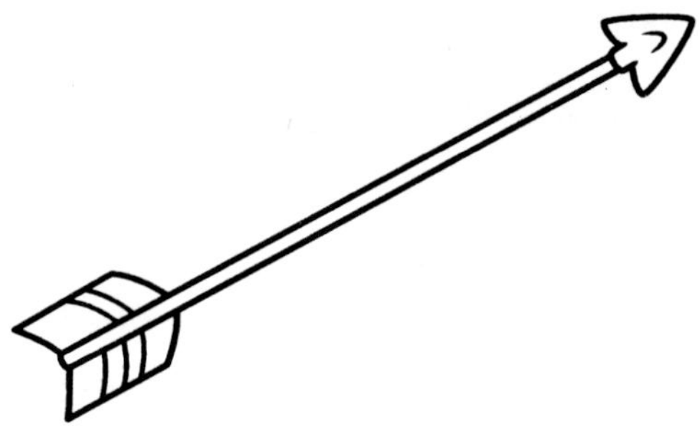

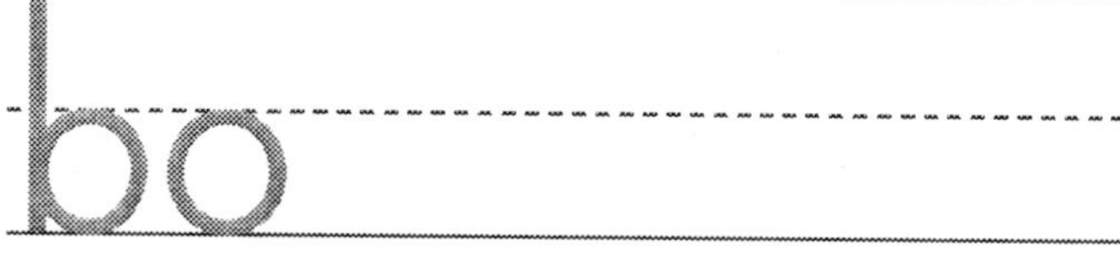 bo

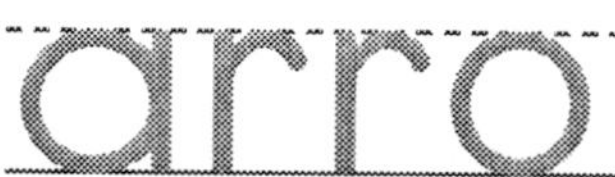 arro

 rainbo

 windo

Name: _______________________

Ends with Xx

Directions: Circle the items that end with the **x sound**. Cross out the other items.

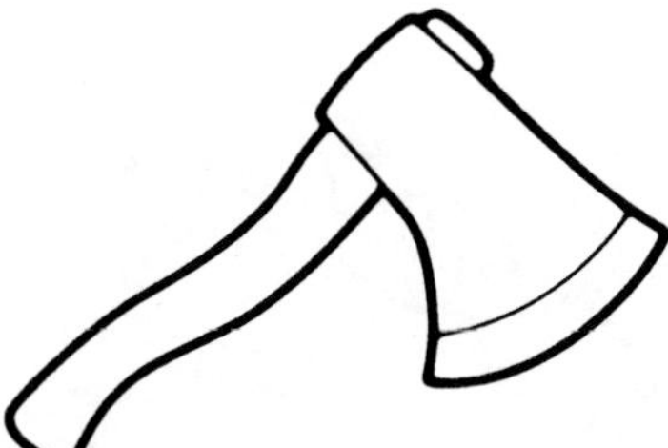  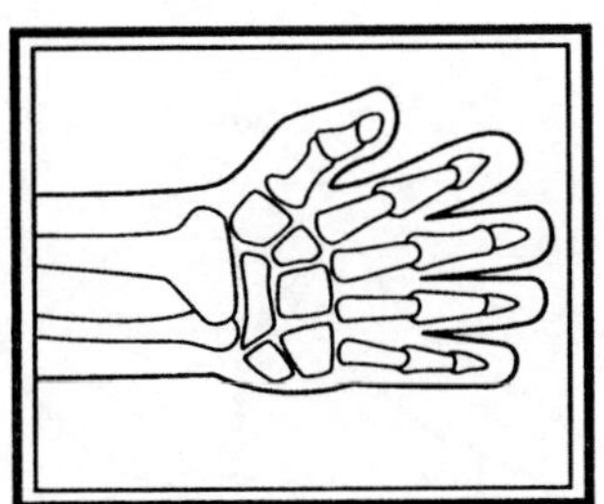

Directions: Read and trace the words to label each item. <u>Underline</u> the **X**s.

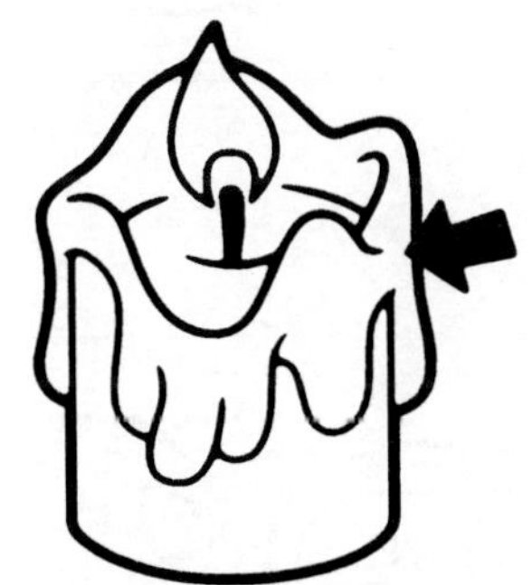  

wax   sax   T. rex

Directions: Circle the number of syllables in **Ty-ran-no-sau-rus rex**. Clap it.

1　2　3　4　5　6　7　8　9　10

Name: _______________________

Ss, Tt, or Xx?

Directions: Listen to the ending sound for each item. Write the ending letter to complete each word. Trace the other letters and read the word.

a___    bu___    je___

fo___    sa___    ra___

ba___    si___    ga___

Name: _______________________________

Choose the Ending

Directions: Fill in the circle that has the letter for the **ending sound** for each item.

b g d w	n m r s	m d l p
m n p r	d t p b	n m g w
s t w x	l n m p	g m n s

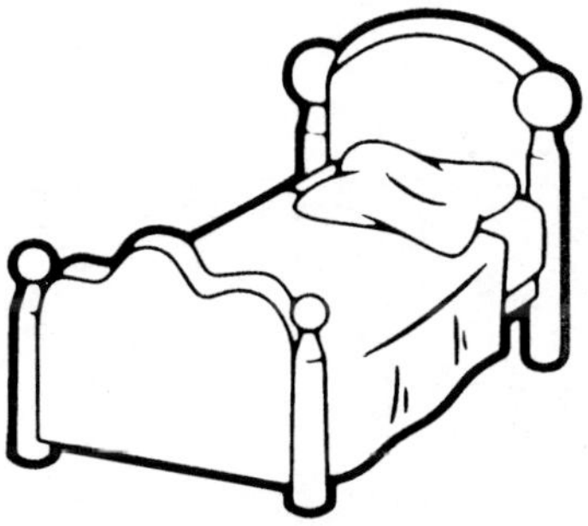

Name: _______________________

Match It or Cross It Out

Directions: Circle the two items that end with the letter at the top of each box. Cross out the item that has a different ending.

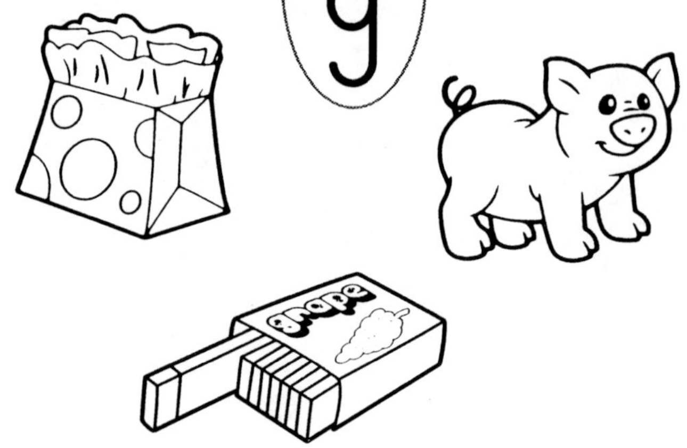

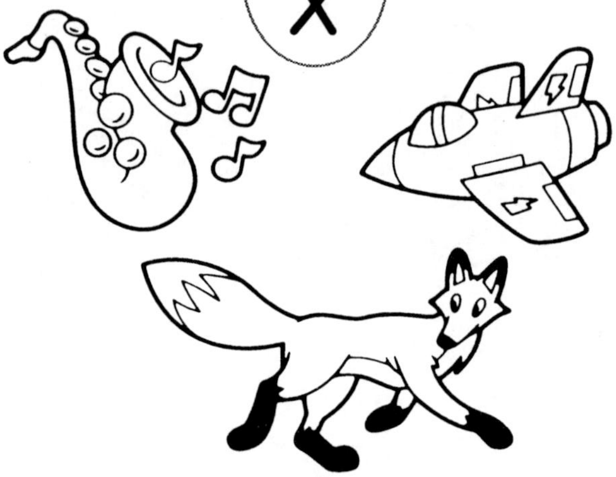

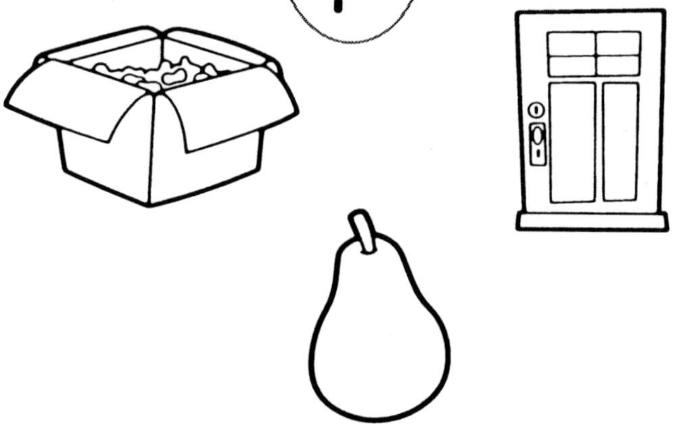

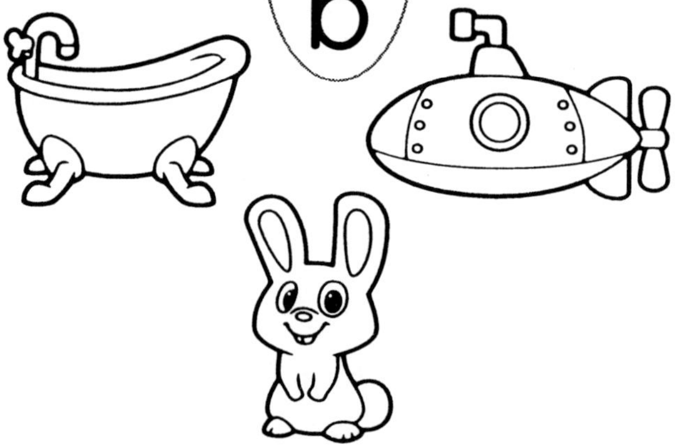

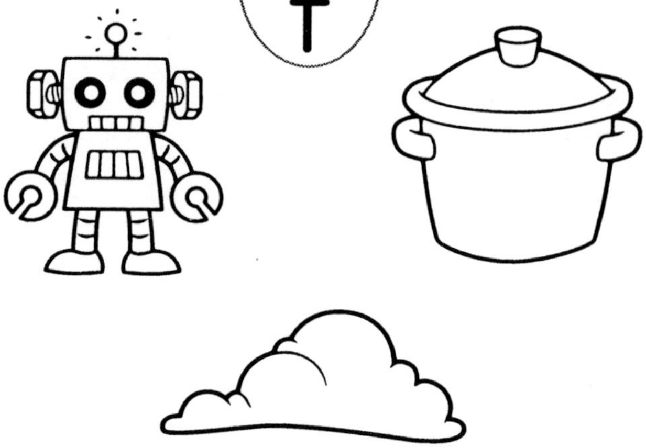

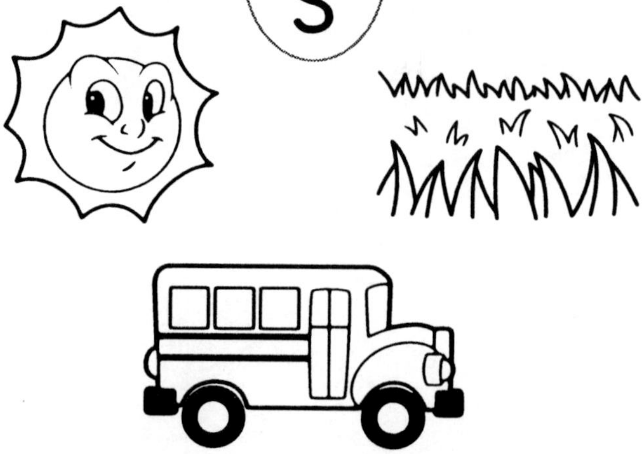

Name: _______________________________

Short A Sound

Directions: Add an **a** to the middle of each pair of letters to make a **short a** word. Read the words with the **short a sound**.

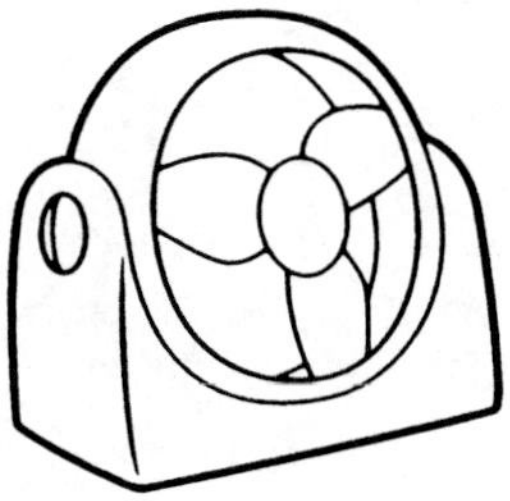

f ___ n 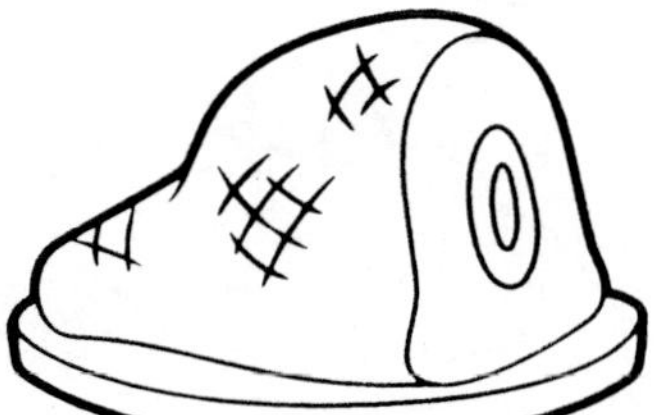   h ___ m 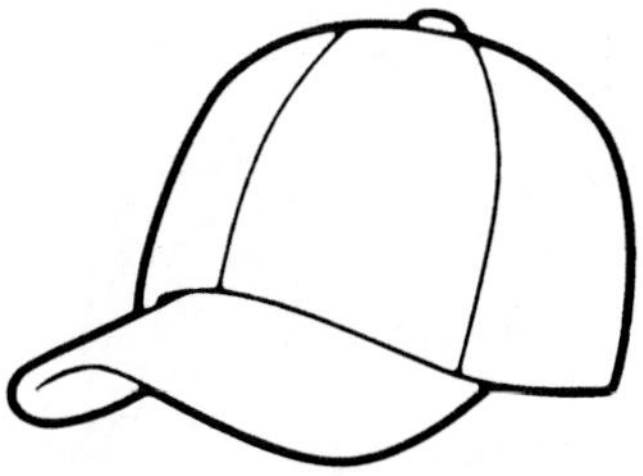   c ___ p

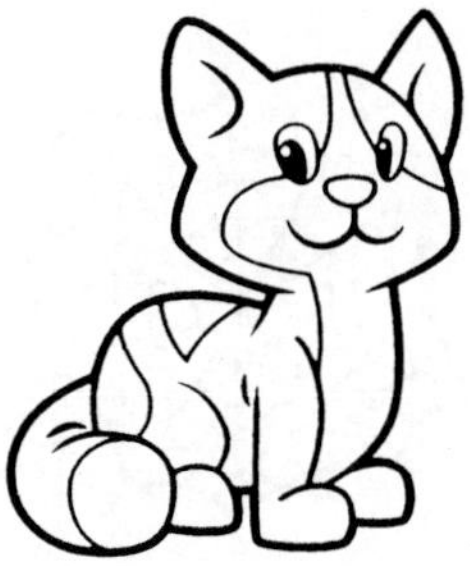

c ___ t 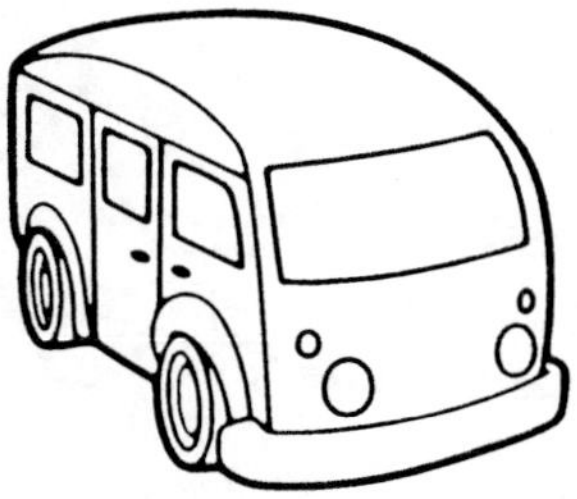   v ___ n 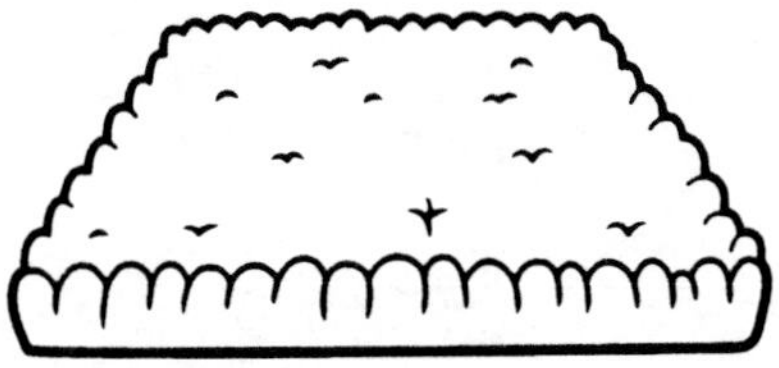   m ___ t

Directions: Count and clap 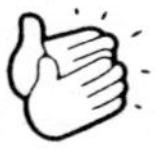 the syllables in each word that has a **short a** sound. Trace the word. Then, circle the number of syllables.

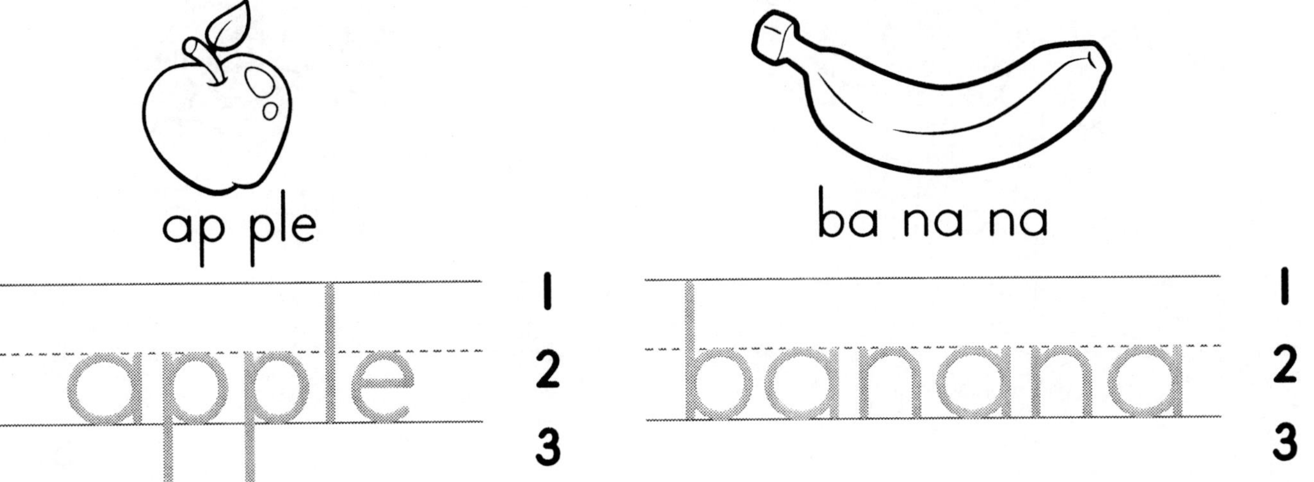

Name: _______________________________

Short E Sound

Directions: Add an **e** to the middle of each pair of letters to make a **short e** word. Read the words with the **short e sound**.

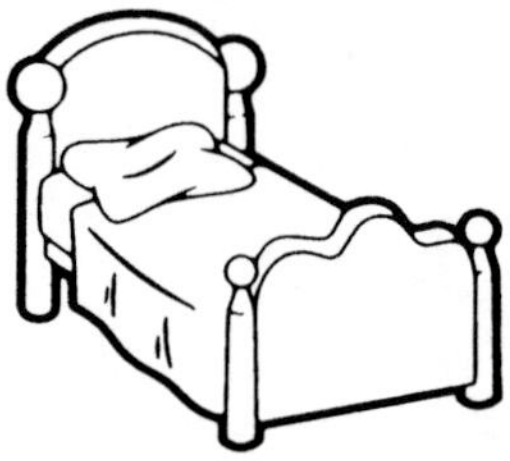

b___d    j___t    m___n

h___n   n___g    w___b

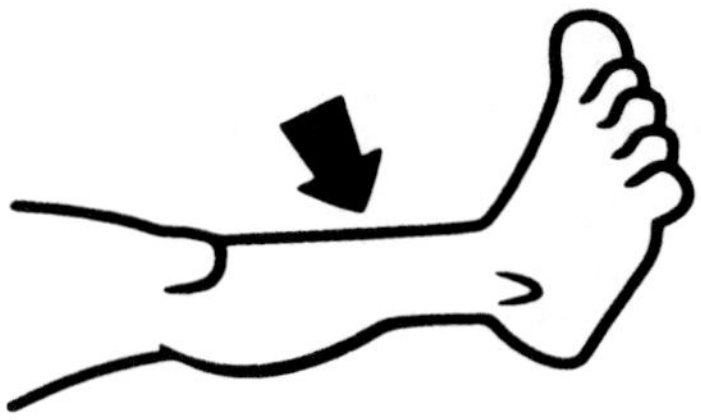

Directions: Count and clap  the syllables in each word that has a **short e** sound. Trace the word. Then, circle the number of syllables.

el e phant

elephant   1 2 3

elf

elf   1 2 3

Name: _________________________________

Short I Sound

Directions: Add an **i** to the middle of each pair of letters to make a **short i** word. Read the words with the **short i sound**.

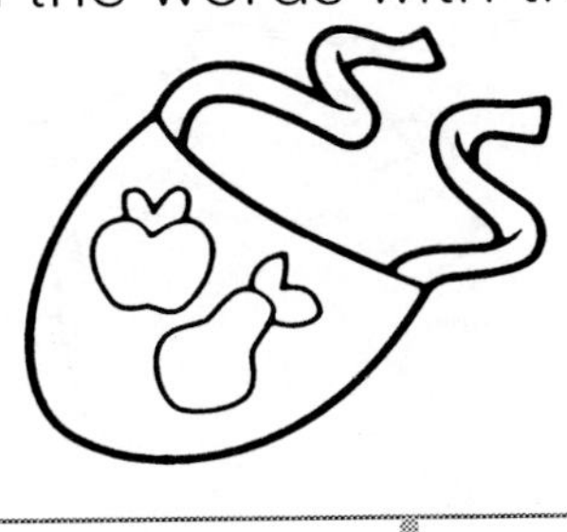

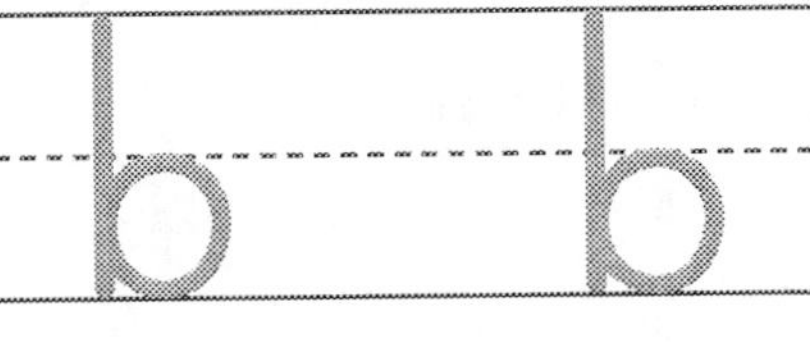

b ___ b

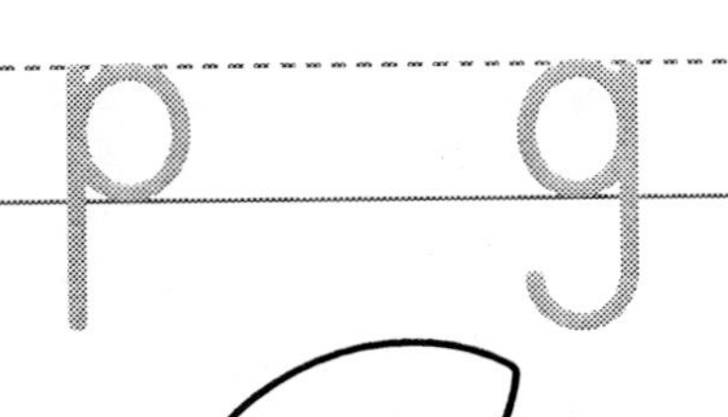

p ___ g

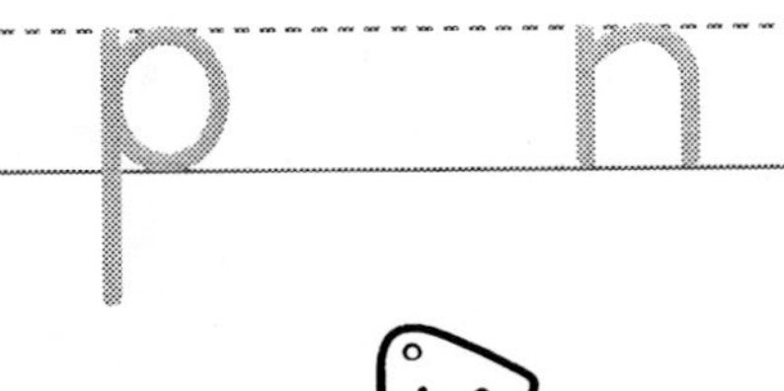

p ___ n

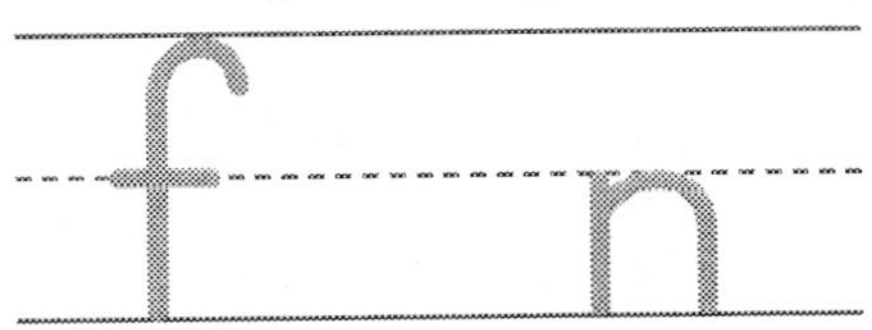

f ___ n

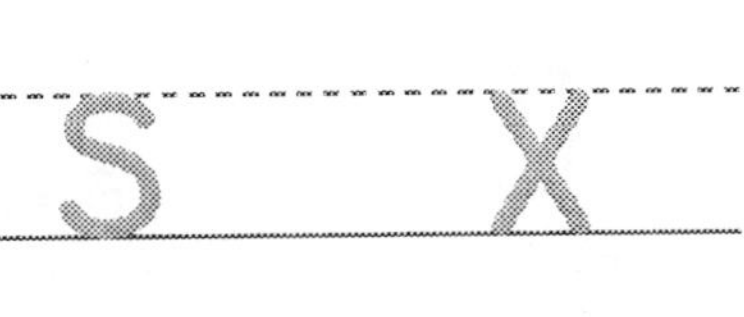

s ___ x

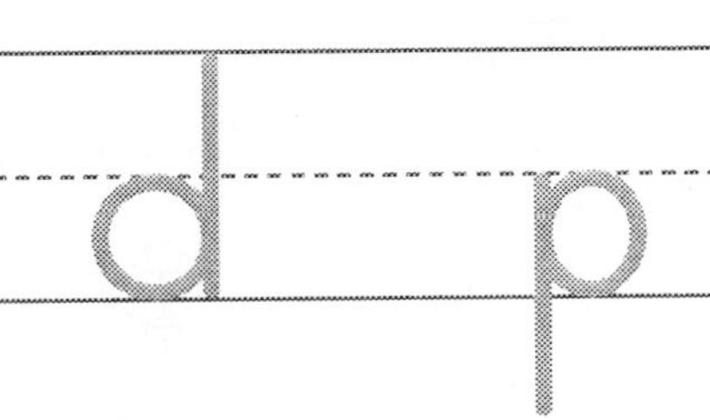

d ___ p

Directions: Count and clap 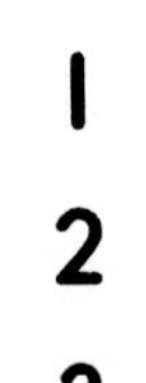 the syllables in each word that has a **short i** sound. Trace the word. Then, circle the number of syllables.

kit ten

kitten

1
2
3

mix er

mixer

1
2
3

Name: ___________________________________

Short O Sound

Directions: Add an **o** to the middle of each pair of letters to make a **short o** word. Read the words with the **short o sound**.

d o g   t o p   p o t

m o p   b o x   m o m

Directions: Count and clap the syllables in each word that begins with a **short o** sound. Trace the word. Then, circle the number of syllables.

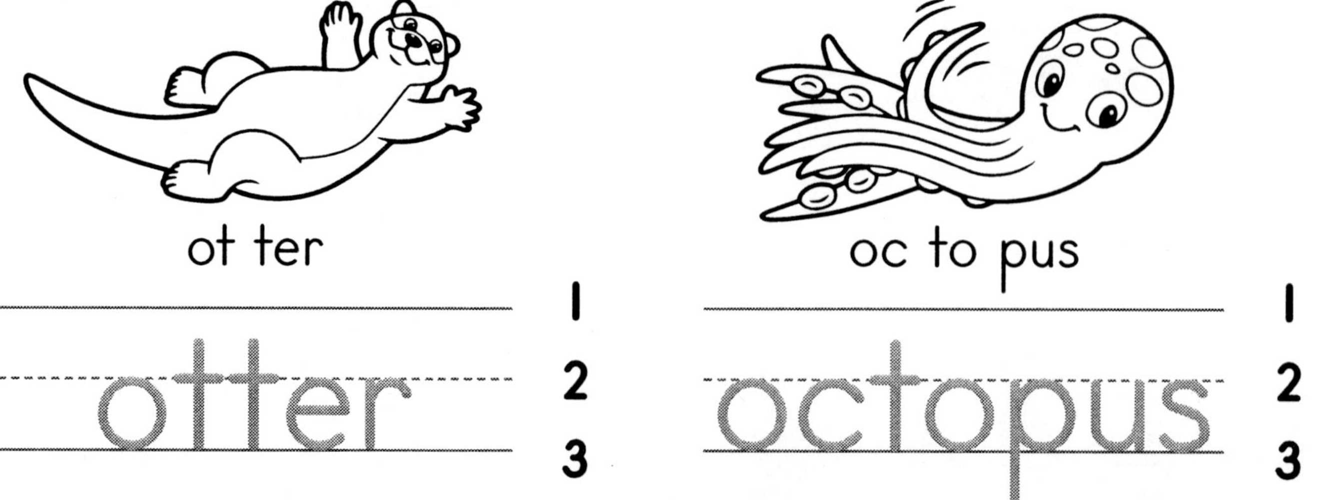

ot ter

otter

1
2
3

oc to pus

octopus

1
2
3

Short U Sound

Directions: Add a **u** to the middle of each pair of letters to make a **short u** word. Read the words with the **short u sound**.

b____g   t____b   n____t

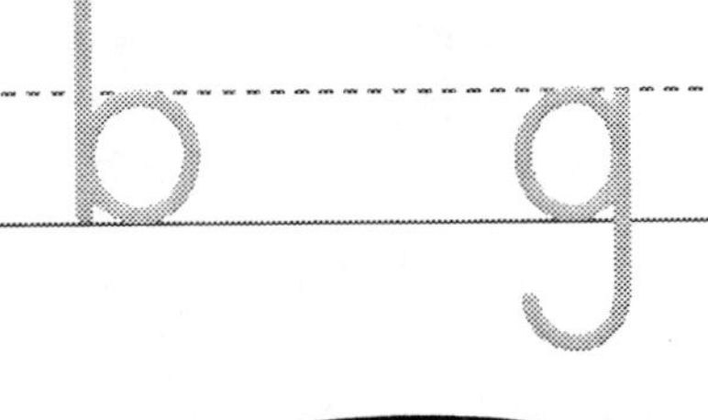

c____p   c____b   s____n

Directions: Count and clap the syllables in each word that begins with a **short u** sound. Trace the word. Then, circle the number of syllables.

um pire

um brel la

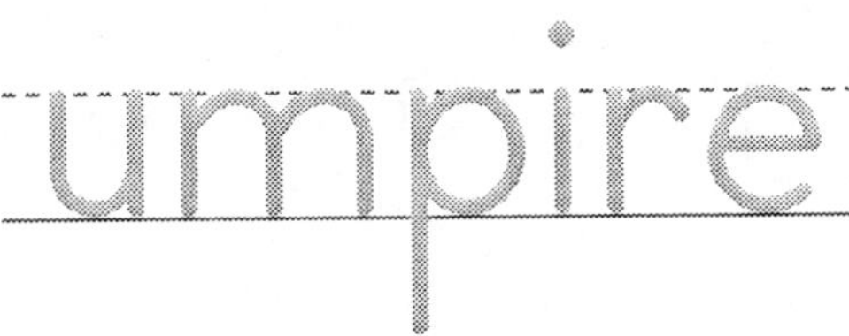
umpire

1
2
3

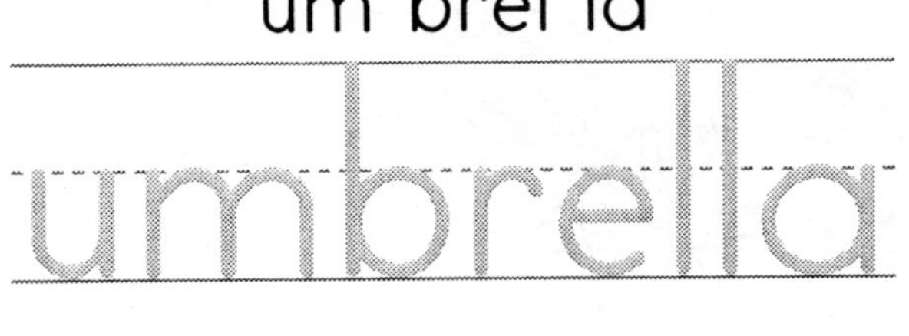
umbrella

1
2
3

Name: _______________________

Choose the Short Vowel

Directions: Say the name of each item. Fill in the circle for its **short vowel sound**.

  a  e  i 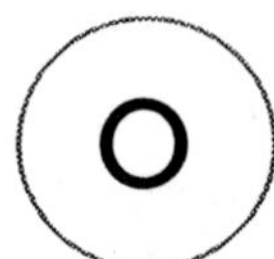 o  u

  a 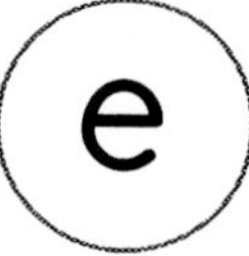 e  i 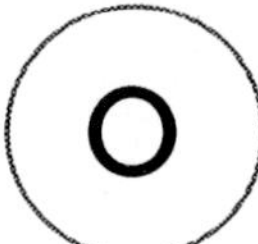 o  u

  a  e  i  o  u

  a  e  i 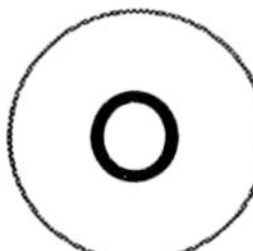 o  u

  a  e  i 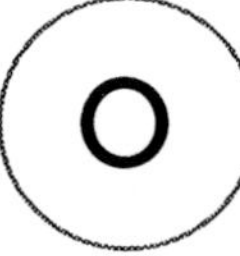 o  u

  a 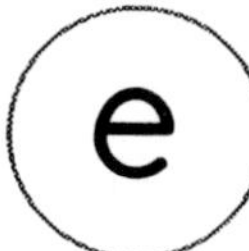 e  i 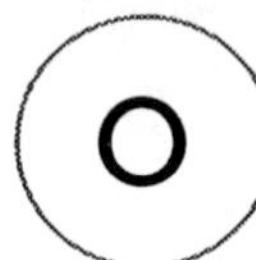 o  u

 a e  i  o  u 

Name: _______________________

Which One Does Not Fit?

Directions: Cross out the item in each row that does not have the **short vowel sound** at the beginning of the row.

a

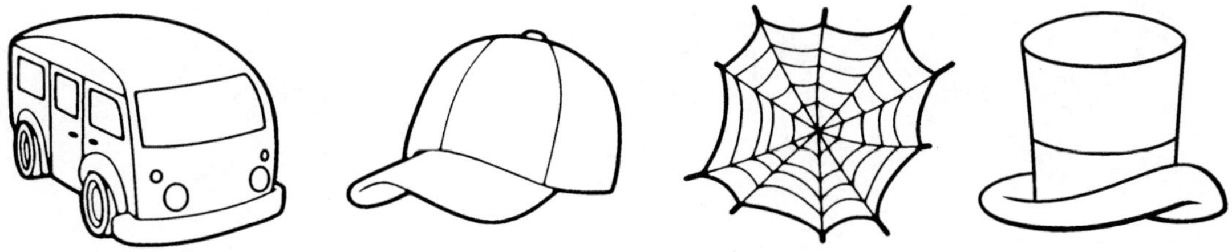

e

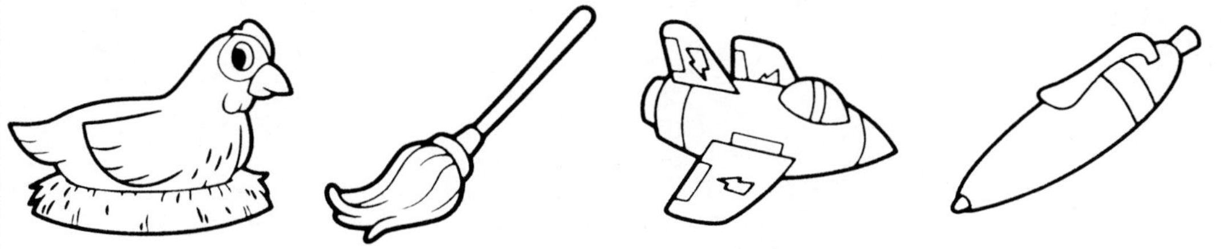

i

o

u

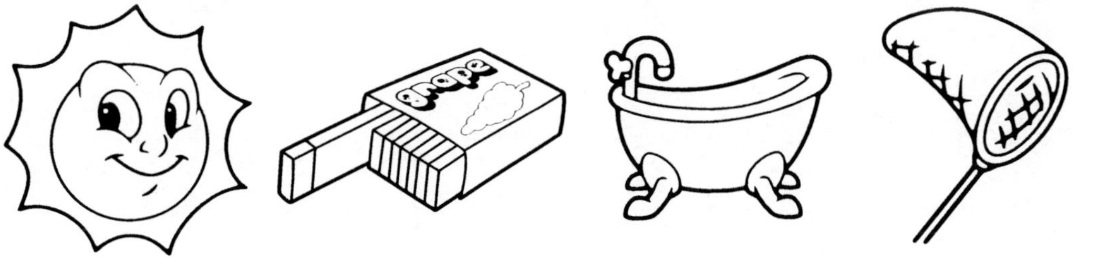

Name: _______________________

Make the Rhymes

Directions: Name each item. Add a short vowel to make rhyming pairs.

b n    s n    b g    m g

f n    c n    f x    b x

j t    n t    p g    w g

Name: _______________________

Find the Rhyming Pair

Directions: Name each item. Draw a line to match each rhyming pair to its short vowel. Name the rhyming pairs.

a

e

i

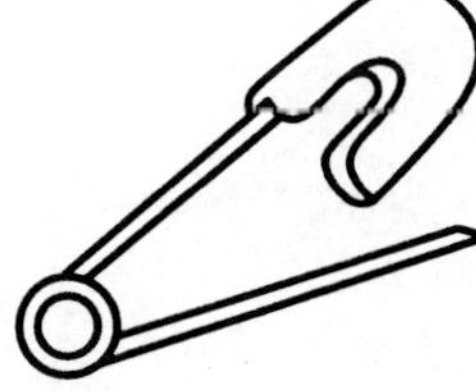

o

u

Name: _______________________

Short A Word Families -am & -ap

Directions: Add the word family endings to the consonants in each row. Read the words for each word family.

am

h   j   r   y

ap

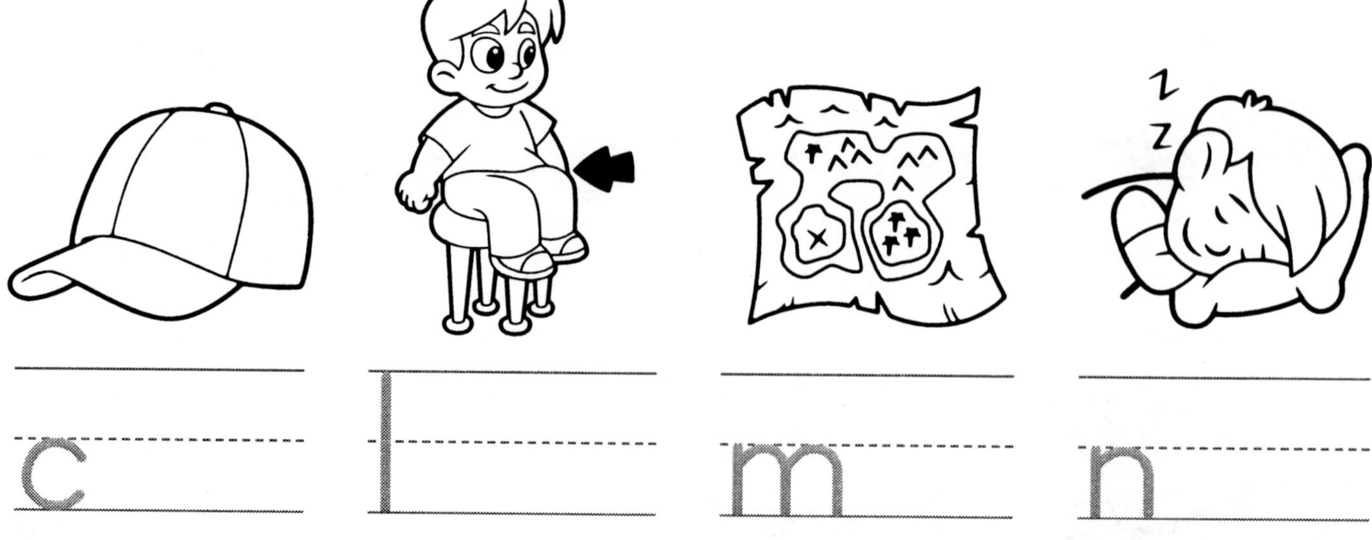

c   l   m   n

Name: _______________________

Short A Word Families -an & -at

Directions: Add a consonant to the beginning of the word family endings in each column. Read the words in each word family.

an	at

Name: _______________________

Short E Word Families -en & -et

Directions: Add a consonant to the beginning of the word family endings in each column. Read the words in each word family.

en

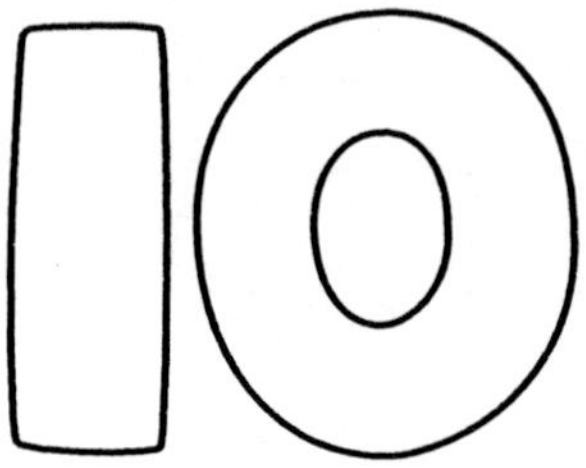

_____ en   _____ en   _____ en   _____ en

et

_____ et   _____ et   _____ et   _____ et

Directions: Add **et** to the beginning letters below. Read the new words.

b___   g___   l___   m___

Name: _______________________________

Short I Word Families -ig & -in

ig

Directions: Use the word wheel to write **ig** words. Read the rhyming words.

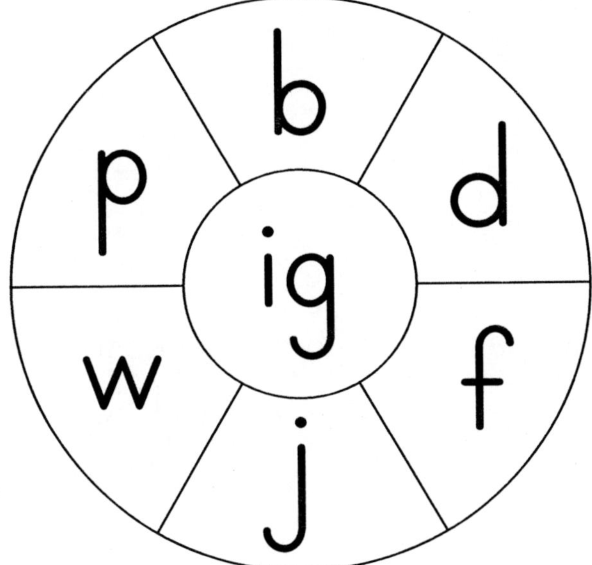

_______________________   _______________________

_______________________   _______________________

_______________________   _______________________

_______________________   _______________________

in

Directions: Add the beginning letter to each **in** word to label the pictures. Read each word.

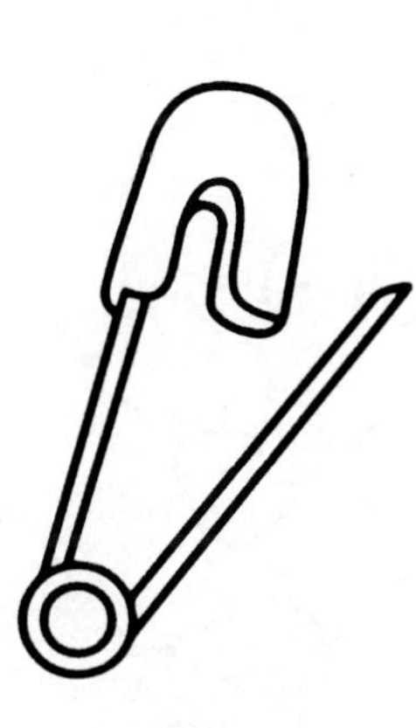         

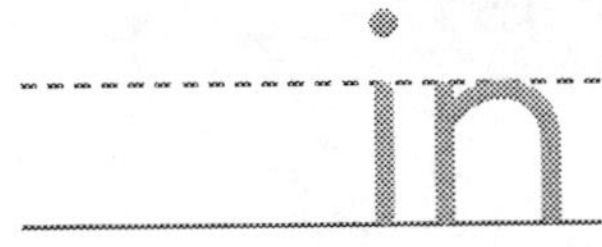   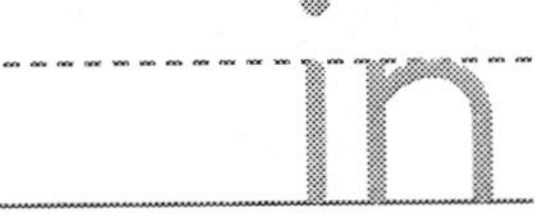   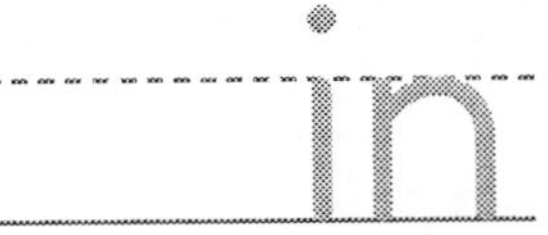   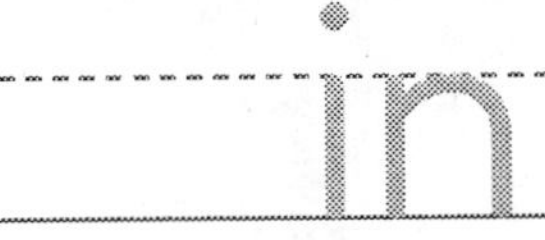

Name: _______________________

Short I Word Family -ip

Directions: Add the beginning letter to each **ip** word. Read the words.

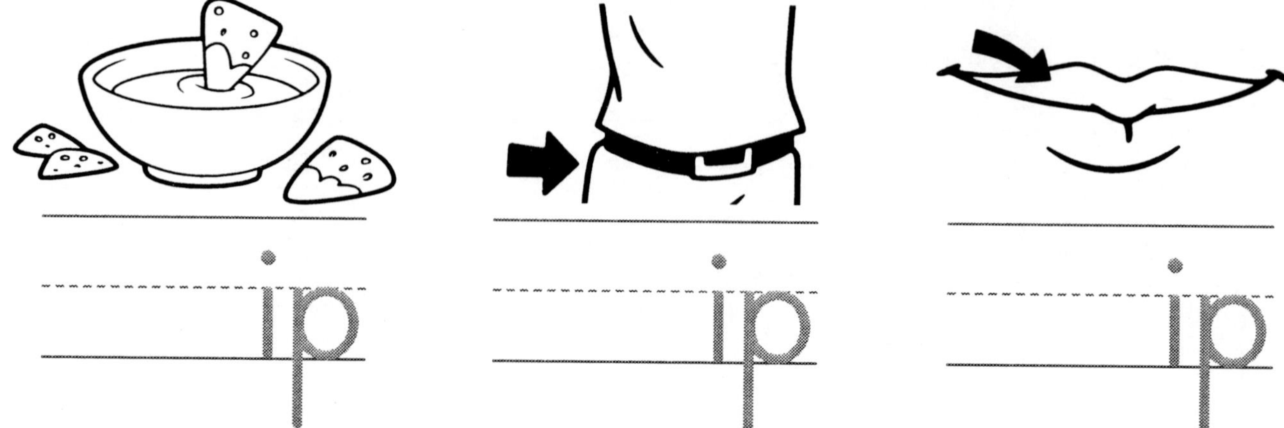

___ip   ___ip   ___ip

Directions: Trace and write the **ip** words. Draw lines to match the words to the pictures.

zip ___

rip ___

sip ___

tip ___

Name: _______________________

Short O Word Families -og & -ot

Directions: Add the word family endings to the consonants in each row. Read the words in each word family.

og

d

h

j

l

ot

c

d

p

h

Directions: Add **ot** to the beginning letters below. Read the new words.

g

n

t

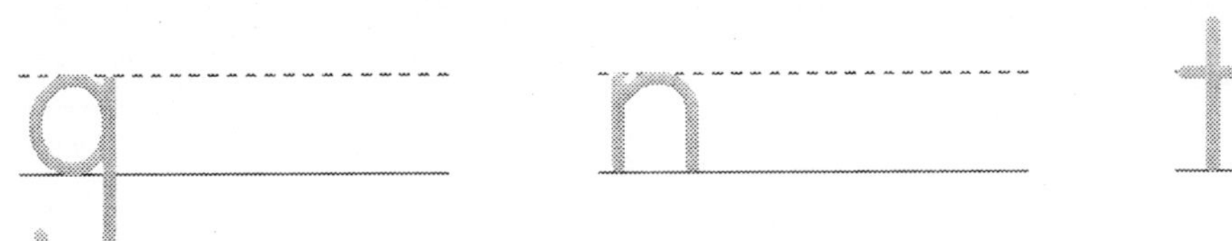

Name: _______________________

Short U Word Families -ub & -ug

ub

Directions: Use one of the **ub** words to label each picture. Read the words.

sub tub rub cub

ug

Directions: Use the word wheel to make **ug** words. Read the words.

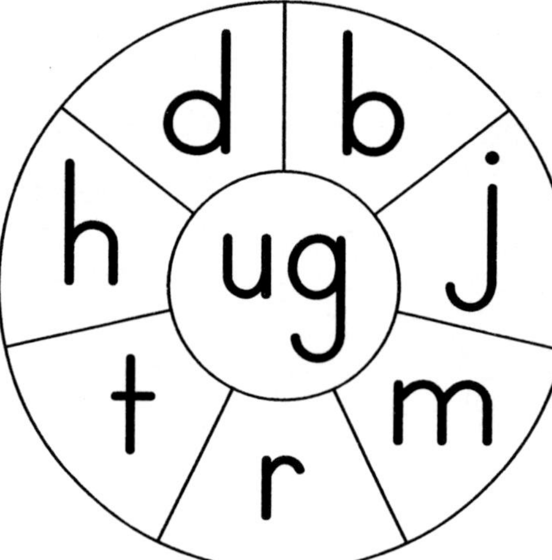

Name: _______________________

Double L Word Families

Directions: Add the word endings to the consonants in each column. Read the words in each word family.

all	ell	ill
b	b	b
c	f	d
f	s	f
h	t	h
m	w	m
t	y	w

Name: _______________________________

Find the Word Family Words

Directions: Read and trace each sentence. Then, find and underline three words that are in the same word family in each sentence.

A big pig did a jig.

Frog can jog on a log.

Is Dad sad or mad?

Ned has a red bed.

Run in the sun for fun!

Short Vowel Stories

Directions: Read and trace each story. Add what is missing to each picture.

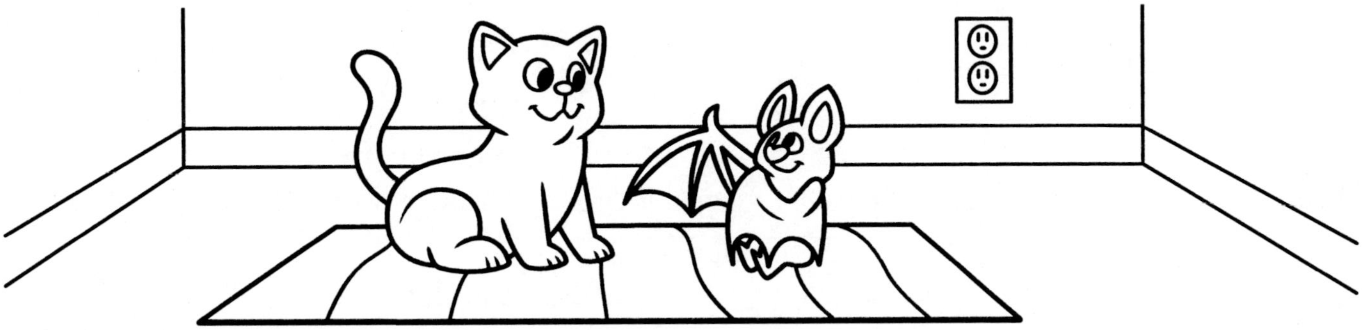

The fat cat had a hat.

He and Bat sat on a mat.

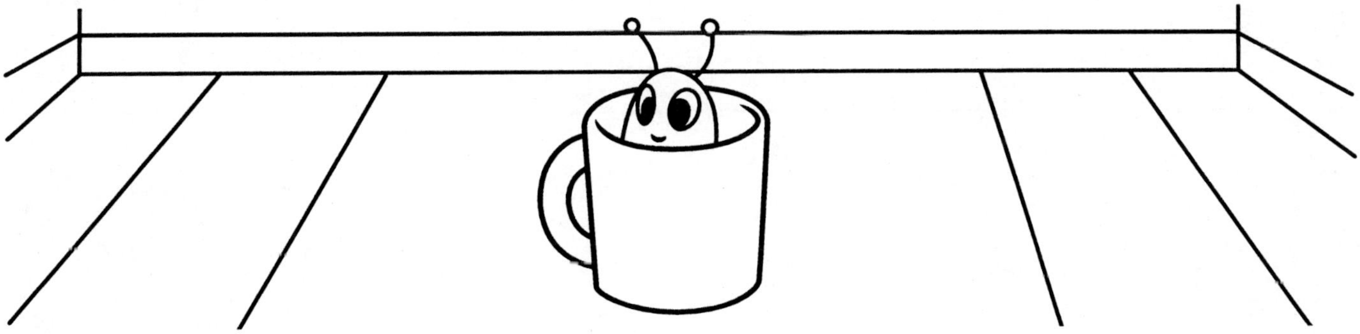

A bug is in the mug.

The mug is on a rug.

Name: ___________________

Shhhh!

The **e** at the end of a word is silent, but it helps the vowel at the beginning say its name.

plan + e = plane

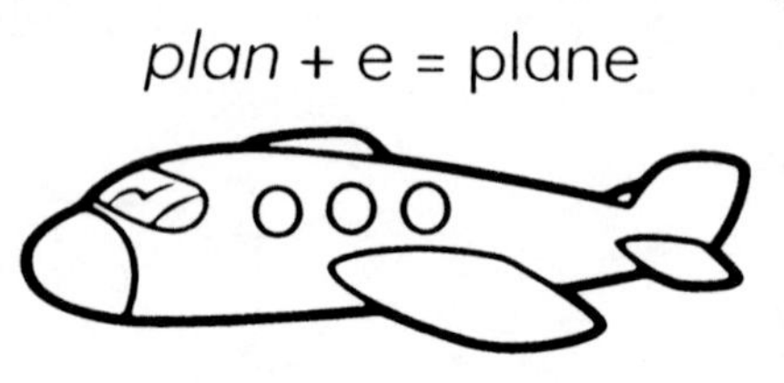

Directions: Add an **e** to each short vowel word to make a new **long vowel** word.

can + e = __________

man + e = __________

tap + e = __________

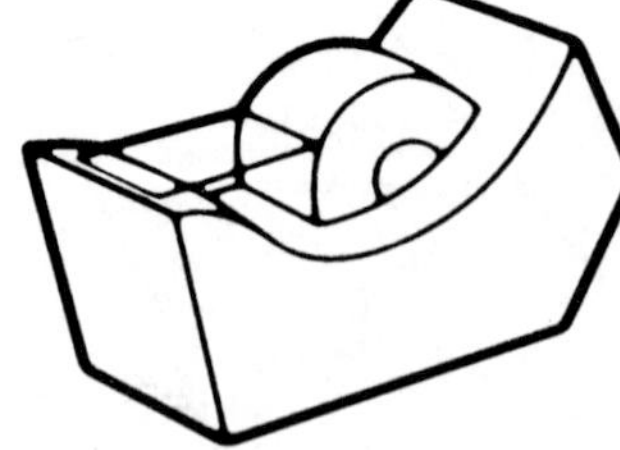

cub + e = __________

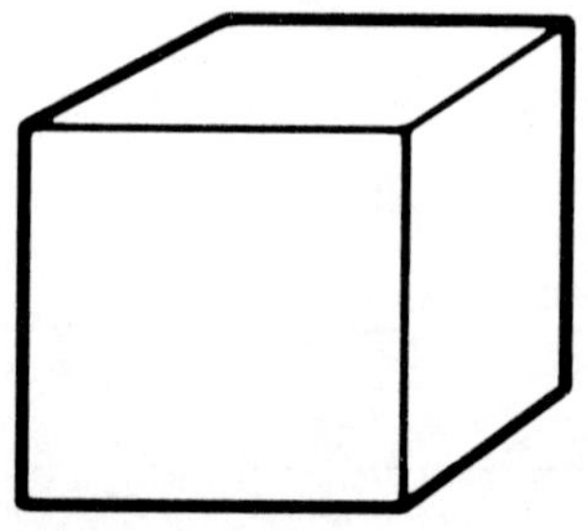

Magic E

Name: _______________________________

Directions: Add an **e** to each short vowel word to make a new **long vowel** word! Read the two words and listen to the different sounds. Then, trace the sentences and circle those two words in it.

cap + e = _______________

She has a cap and a cape.

tub + e = _______________

The tube is in the tub.

hug + e = _______________

She gave a huge hug!

Name: _______________________

Long A Sound

Directions: The **silent e** is sometimes called a **bossy e** because it tells the first vowel to say its name. Add the **silent e** to the letters below. Trace and read the **long a** words you wrote.

lak	can	rak
cag	tap	vas
gat	rac	cak

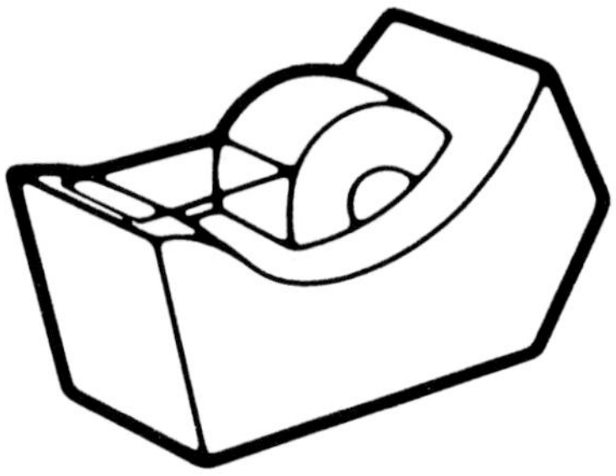

Name: _______________________

Long I Sound

Directions: Long vowels say their names. Add an **i** to the letters below to make **long i** words. Read the words you wrote. Circle the **silent e** in each word.

b _ ke 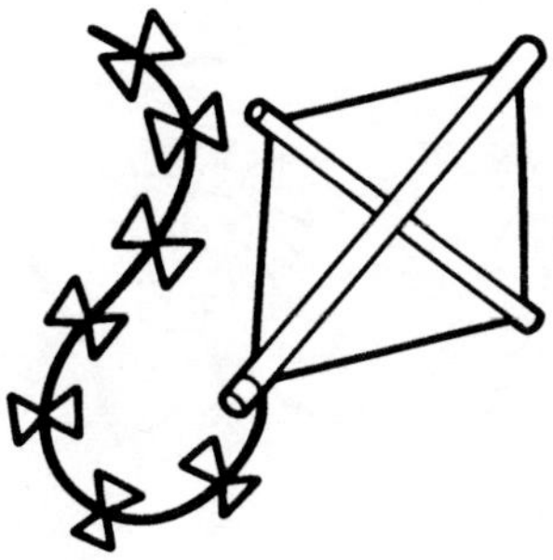   k _ te 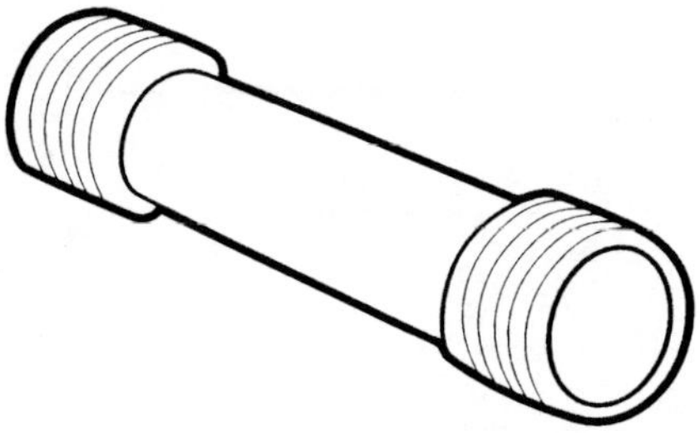   p _ pe

d _ ce    m _ ce 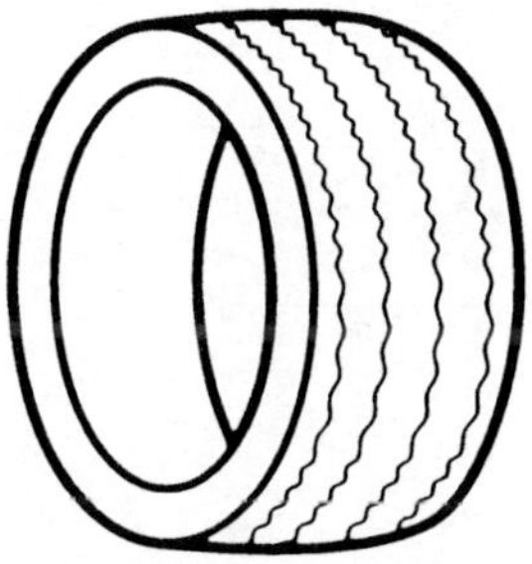   t _ re

f _ re 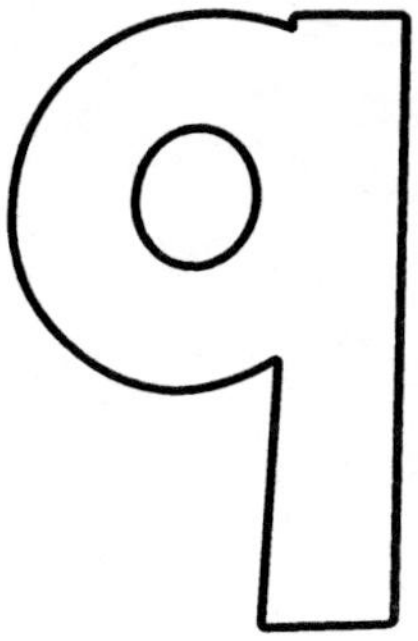   n _ ne    v _ ne

Name: ________________________________

Long O Sound

Directions: Add an **o** to the letters below to make **long o** words. Trace and read the words you wrote. Circle the **silent e** in each word.

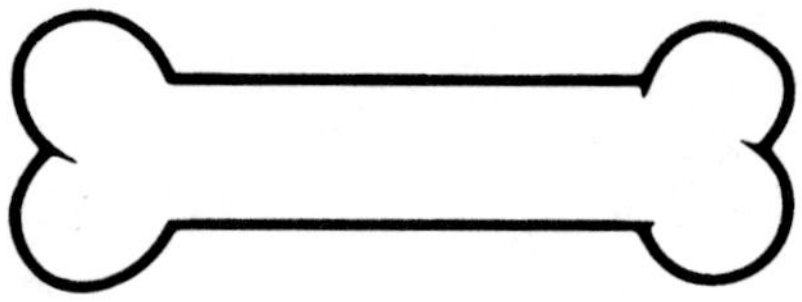

b_ne   r_be   d_me

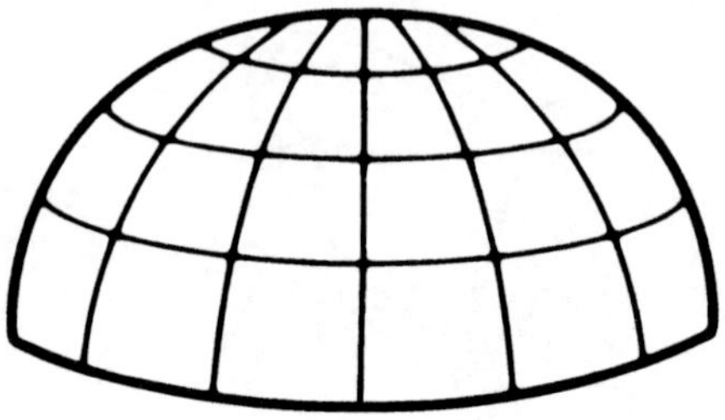

r_pe   n_se   c_ne

h_se

Directions: Add a **long o** to each letter to write three sight words. Read the sight words.

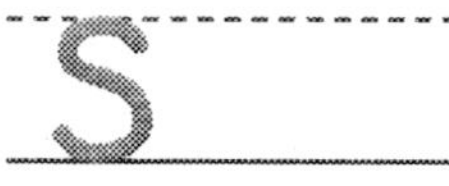

s____

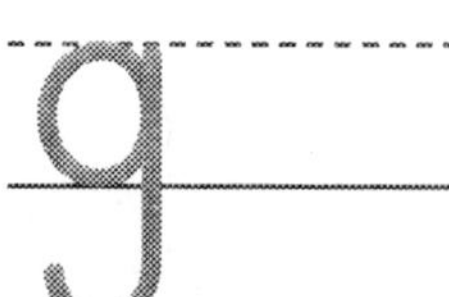

g____

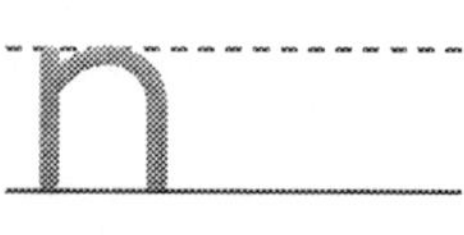

n____

Name: ________________________

Long U Sound

Directions: Add a **u** to the letters below to make **long u** words. Trace and read the words you wrote. Circle the **silent e** in each word.

m _ l e   t _ n e   c _ b e

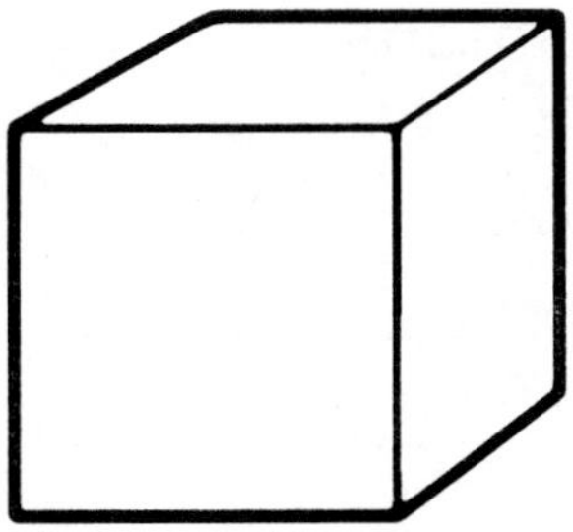

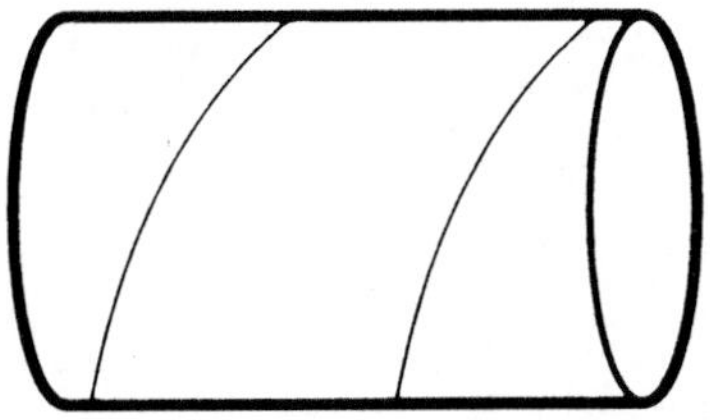

t _ b e   d _ n e   J _ n e

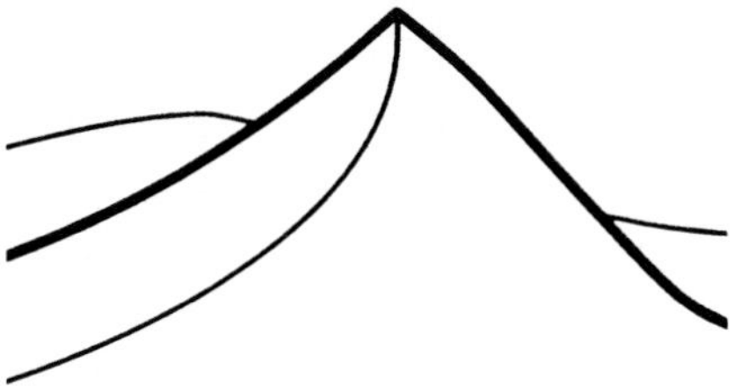

Directions: Trace the sentence and circle the two **long u** words.

That mule is cute!

Name: _______________________

Y Can Be a Vowel

Some words that end in **y** do not have another vowel. In two-letter and three-letter words without a vowel, the **y** is the vowel. It sounds like a **long i**.

Directions: Add a **y** to each letter and then write the two sight words!

m__ _______   b__ _______

Directions: Add a **y** to each group of letters. Trace and read each word. Read all the words you made when you added a **y**!

cr____   dr____   fl____

fr____   sh____   sk____

Directions: Add a **y** to write three more words. Circle the vowel in each word.

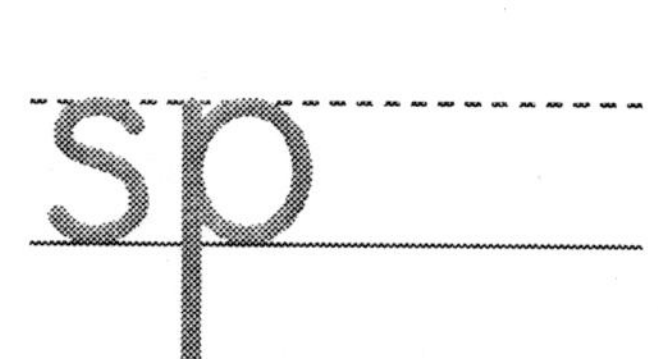

sp____

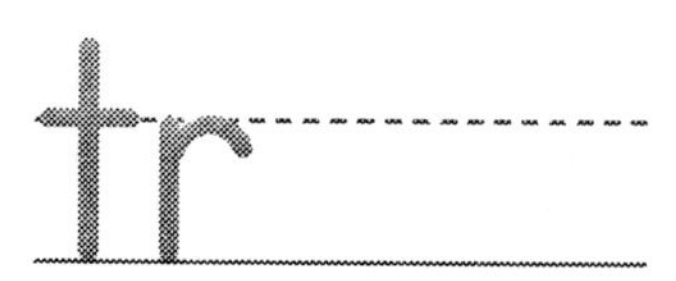

tr____

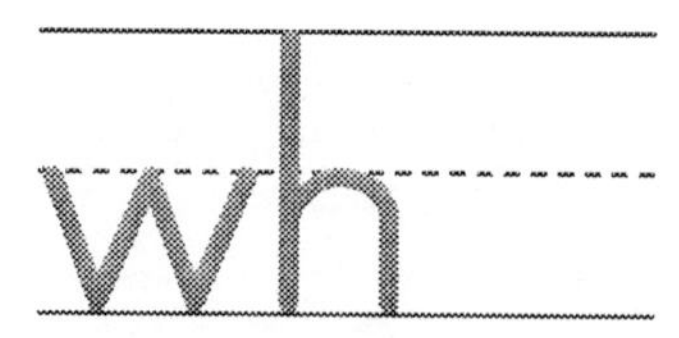

wh____

Name: ___________________________

Choose the Long Vowel

Directions: Name each item and fill in the circle for its **long vowel sound**.

  a  e  i 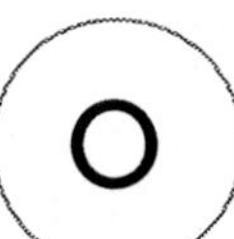 o  u

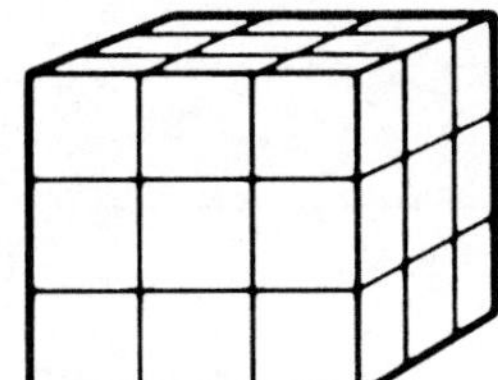  a  e  i  o  u

  a 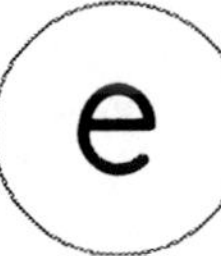 e  i 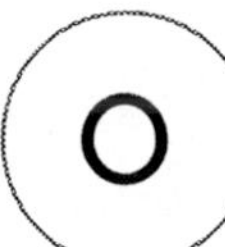 o  u

  a 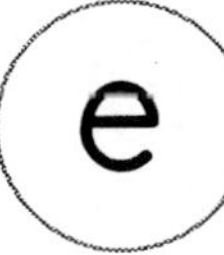 e  i  o  u

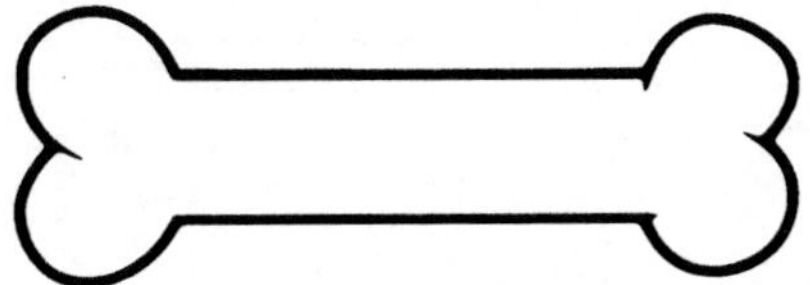  a  e  i 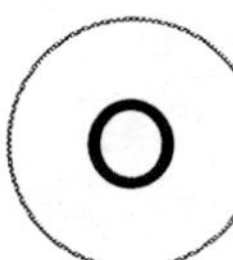 o  u

Name: _______________________

Write the Long Vowel

Directions: Fill in the **long vowel** to complete each word. Read the words.

v _ se

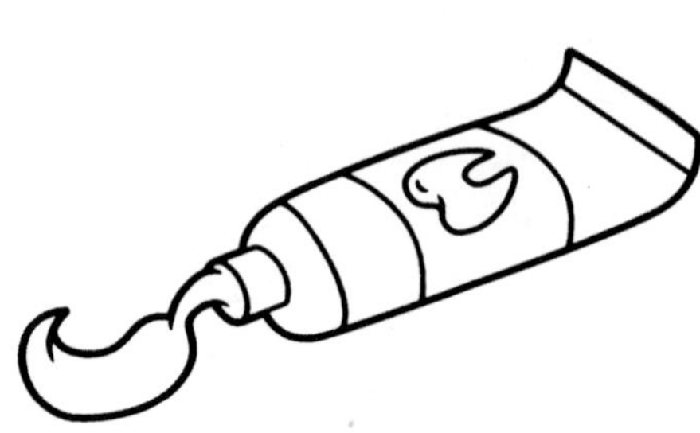

t _ be

r _ be

c _ ne

p _ ne

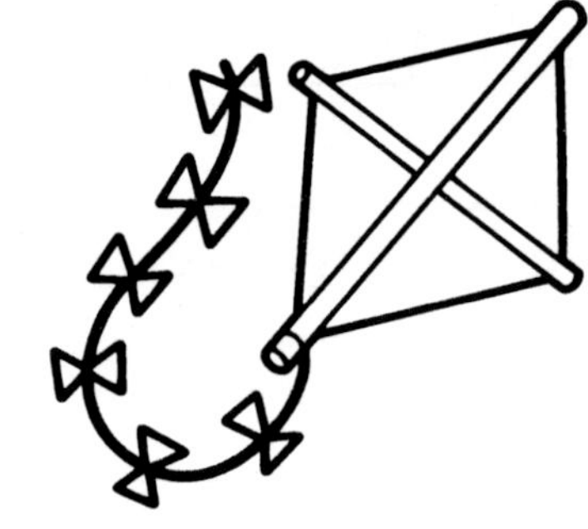

k _ te

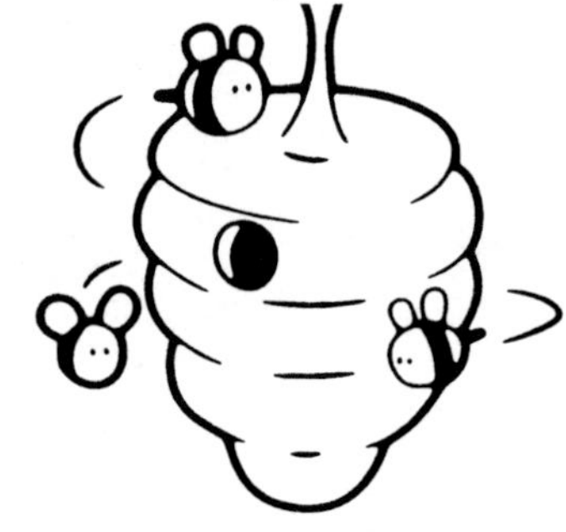

h _ ve

m _ le

c _ ge

Name: _______________________

Match the Rhymes

Directions: Draw a line to match each rhyming pair to its **long vowel sound**.

a  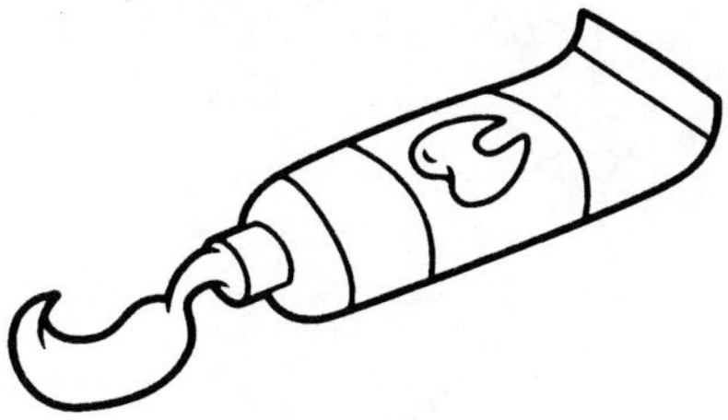
i 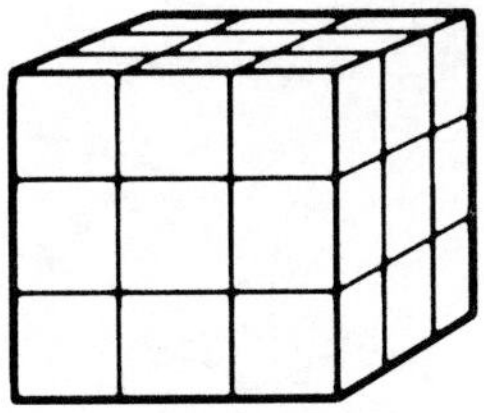 
o  
u

Directions: Write a beginning consonant to make rhyming pairs in each row.

___ice   ___ice

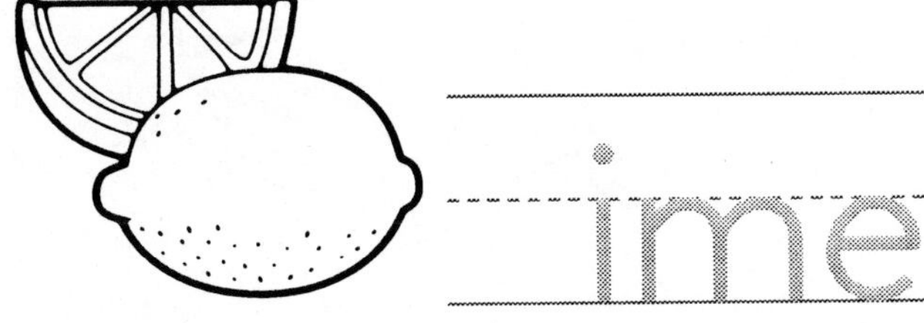

___ime   ___ime

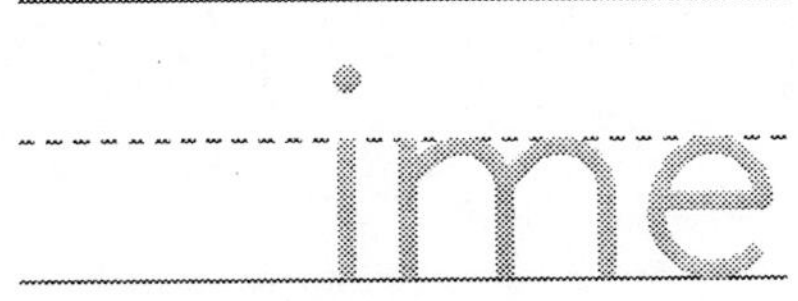

More Rhymes

Directions: Circle the two items in each box that rhyme. Cross out the other item.

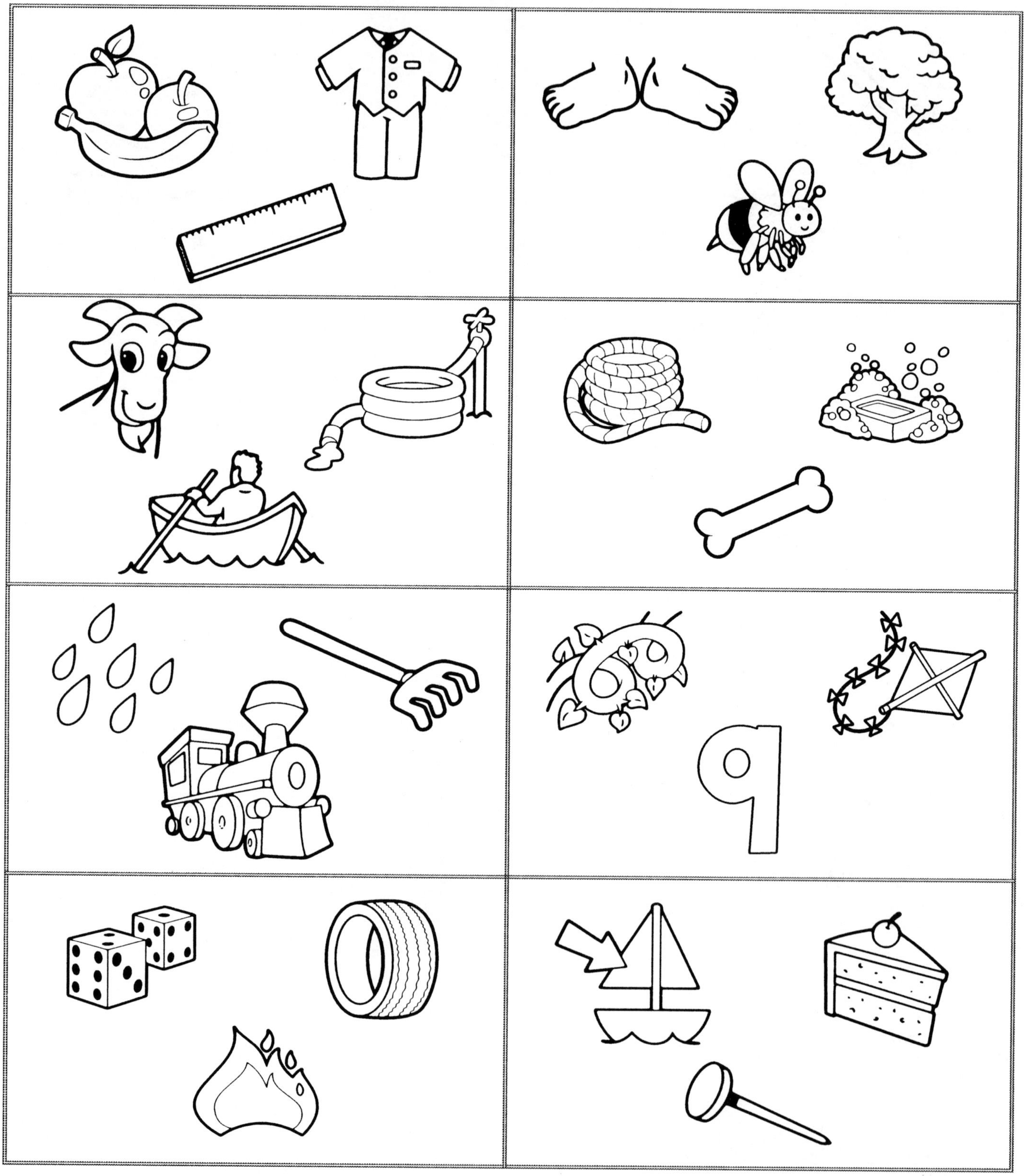

Name: ___________________________

Find the Long Vowel Rhymes

Directions: Read and trace the words. Circle the two rhyming words you hear.

Mice play with dice.

Bake a cake with me.

Is it a tube or a cube?

Name: _______________________

Long A Word Family -ake

Directions: Add the **ake** word family ending to each consonant. Read the rhyming words.

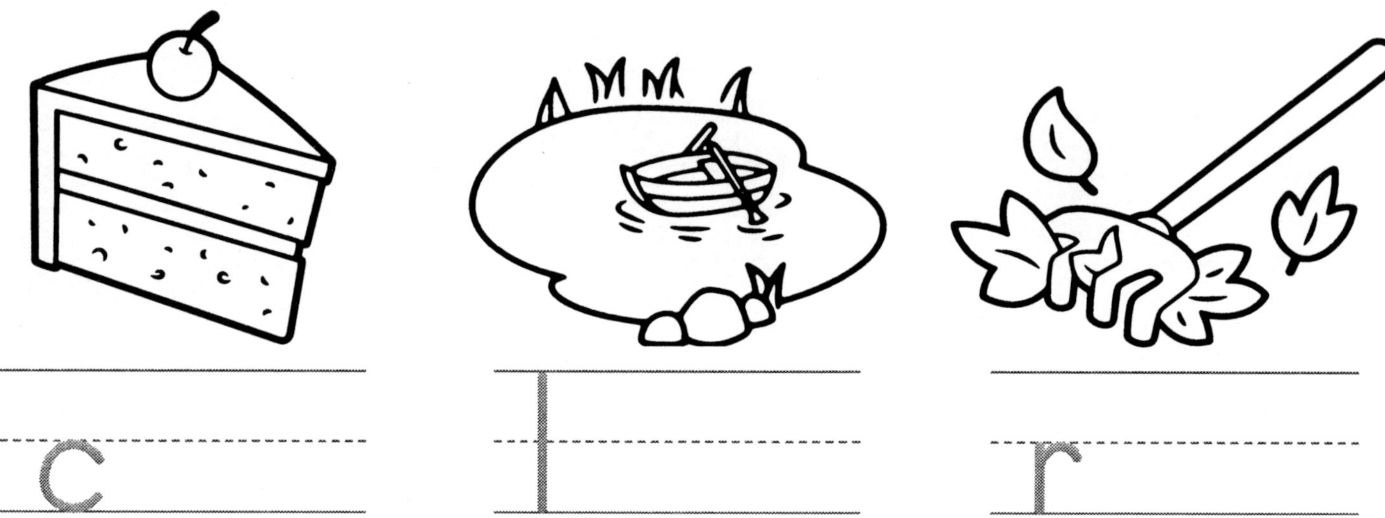

c _______________________

l _______________________

r _______________________

Directions: Choose words that end in **ake** to complete each sentence. Read each sentence.

(bake   cake   take   wake)

She will _________________ me up today.

We will _________________ a _________________.

I will _________________ the rake to Dad.

Name: ___________________________

Long I Word Families -ice & -ide

ice

Directions: Add a beginning letter to complete each word. Trace and read the rhyming words.

ide

Directions: Add the **ide** word family ending to each consonant. Read the rhyming words.

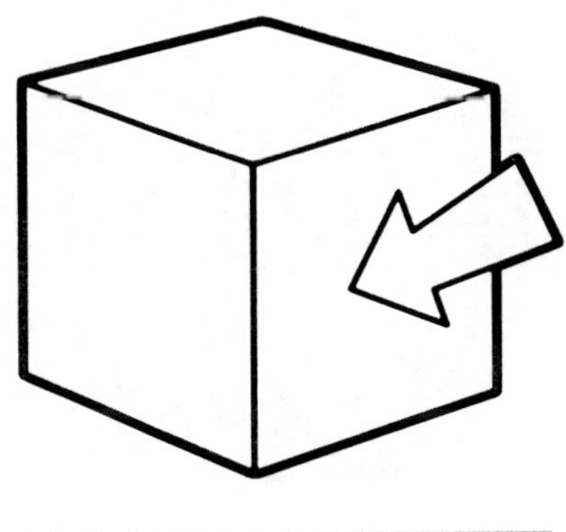

h ______   r ______   s ______

Name: _______________________

Long I Word Families -ime & -ire

ime

Directions: Add a beginning letter to complete each word. Trace and read the rhyming words.

 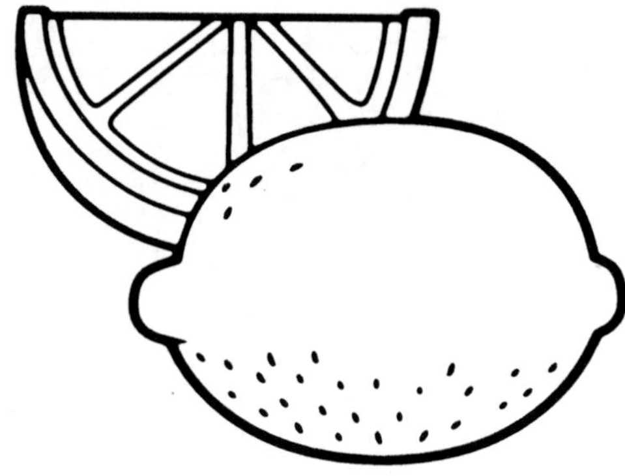 

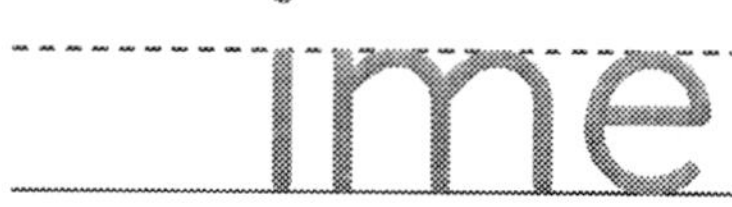  

_____ime   _____ime   _____ime

ire

Directions: Add the **ire** word family ending to each consonant. Read the rhyming words you made.

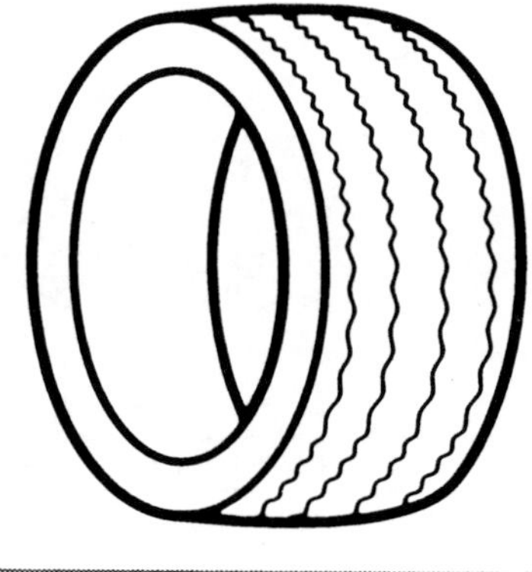  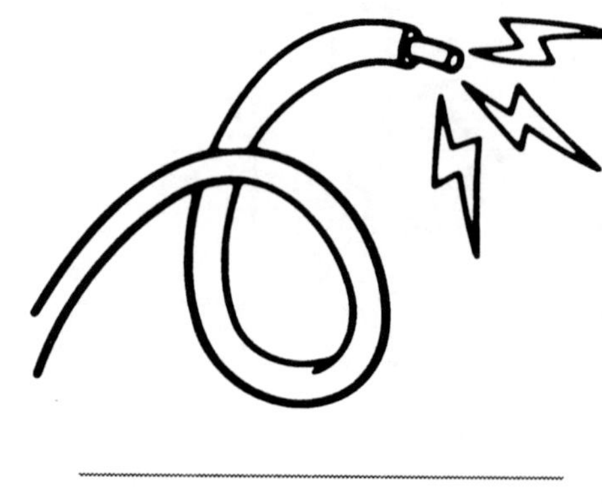

t_____   f_____   w_____

Name: _______________________________

Long O Word Families -ole & -ow

ole

Directions: Add the **ole** word family ending to each consonant. Read the rhyming words you made.

  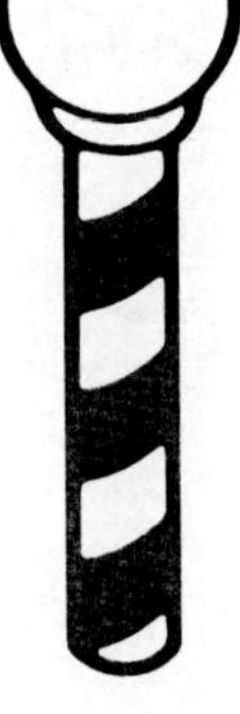

h ________   m ________   p ________

ow

Directions: Use the **ow** words to label each picture. Read each rhyming word.

row   bow   mow   tow

________   ________   ________   ________

Name: _______________________________

Find the Rhymes

Directions: Read and trace each sentence. Circle two rhyming words in each.

A mole is in the hole.

I like to ride my bike.

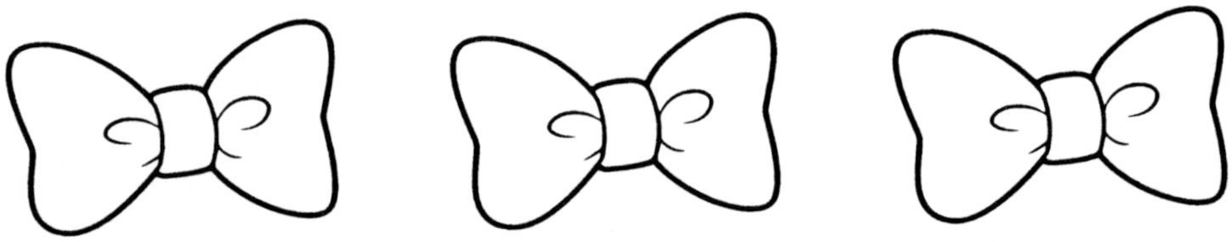

Add a bow to the row.

The fire is in the tire.

Name: _______________________

Finish the Sentences

Directions: Use the long vowel words to finish each sentence. Read your sentences.

tow   time   lake   hide   cone

He will ________________ the car.

She will have a ________________.

What ________________ do you wake up?

May I row in the ________________?

I can ________________ here.

Name: _______________________

Br and Cr Blends

br

Directions: Listen to the beginning sounds of each item. Circle the items that begin with the **br blend**. Cross out the other items.

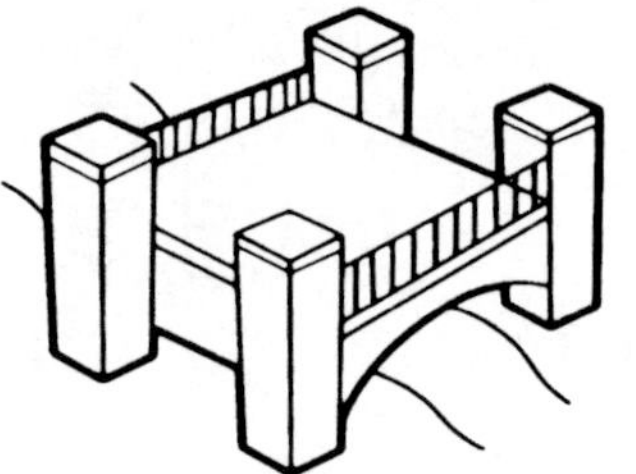 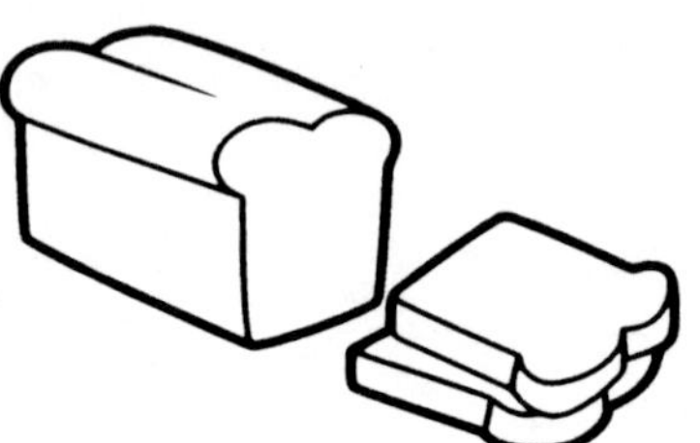 

cr

Directions: Add the **cr blend** to complete each word. Read the words.

___ib

___own

___ab

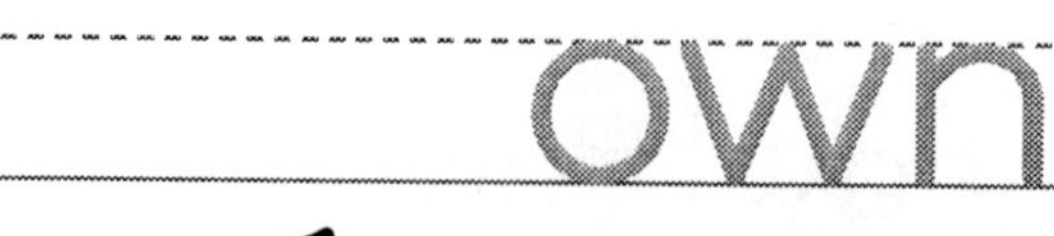

___ow

Name: ___________________________________

Dr and Fr Blends

dr

Directions: Listen to the beginning sounds of each item. Circle the items that begin with the **dr blend**. Cross out the other items.

fr

Directions: Add the **fr blend** to complete each word. Read the words.

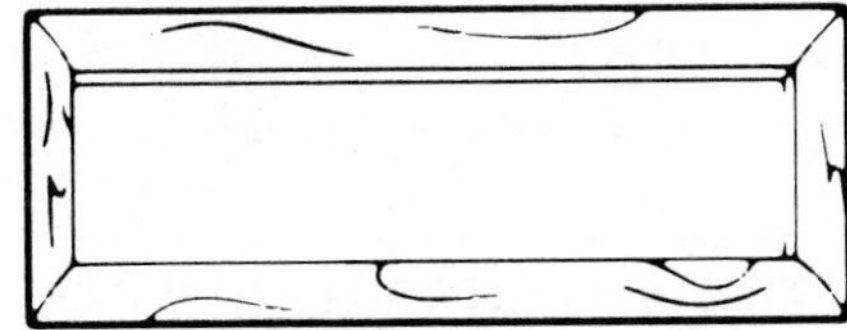

___ og
___ ame

___ own
___ uit

Name: _______________________

Gr and Tr Blends

gr

Directions: Add the **gr blend** to complete each word. Trace and read the words.

 ___ape
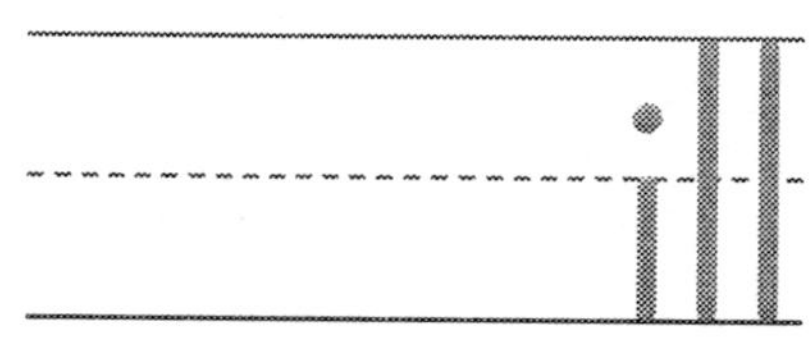 ___ill
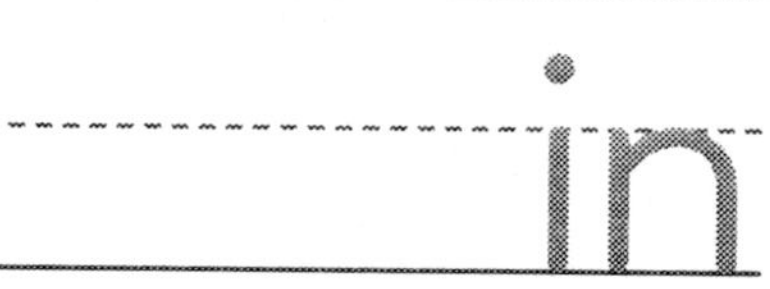 ___in

Directions: Color each crayon the correct color. Circle the blend.

tr

Directions: Listen to the beginning sounds of each item. Circle the items that begin with the **tr blend**. Cross out the other items.

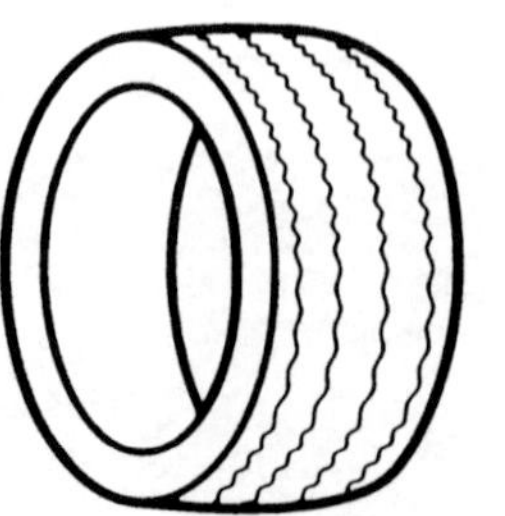

Name: _______________________

R Blends Review

Directions: Listen to the **beginning sounds** for each item. Write the correct blend to complete each word. Read each word.

br cr dr fr gr tr

_____ og	_____ oom
_____ own	_____ apes
_____ ike	_____ ib
_____ um	_____ ame
_____ ab	_____ ill

Name: ___________________________

Bl and Cl Blends

bl

Directions: Add the **bl** blend to complete each word. Trace and read each word.

______ ack

______ ow

______ ock

______ imp

cl

Directions: Listen to the beginning sounds of each item. Circle the items that begin with the **cl blend**. Cross out the other items.

Name: _______________________

Fl and Gl Blends

fl

Directions: Add the **fl blend** to complete each word. Trace and read each word.

___ ag

___ ute

___ ower

___ y

gl

Directions: Listen to the beginning sounds of each item. Circle the items that begin with the **gl blend**. Cross out the other items. Name the items that begin with the **gl blend**.

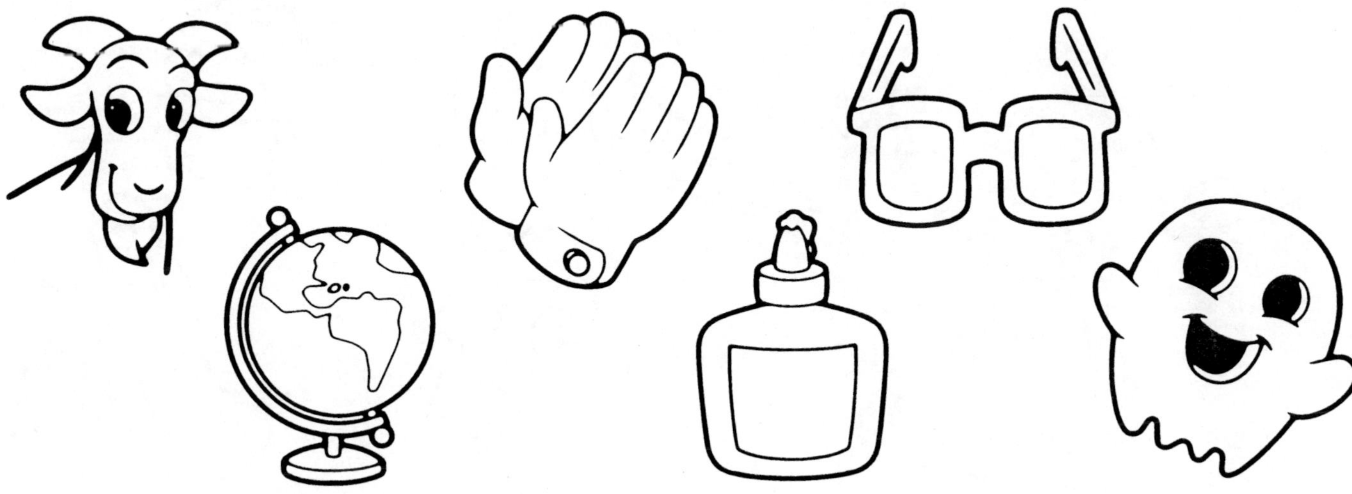

Name: _______________________

Pl and Sl Blends

pl

Directions: Add the **pl blend** to complete each word. Trace and read each word.

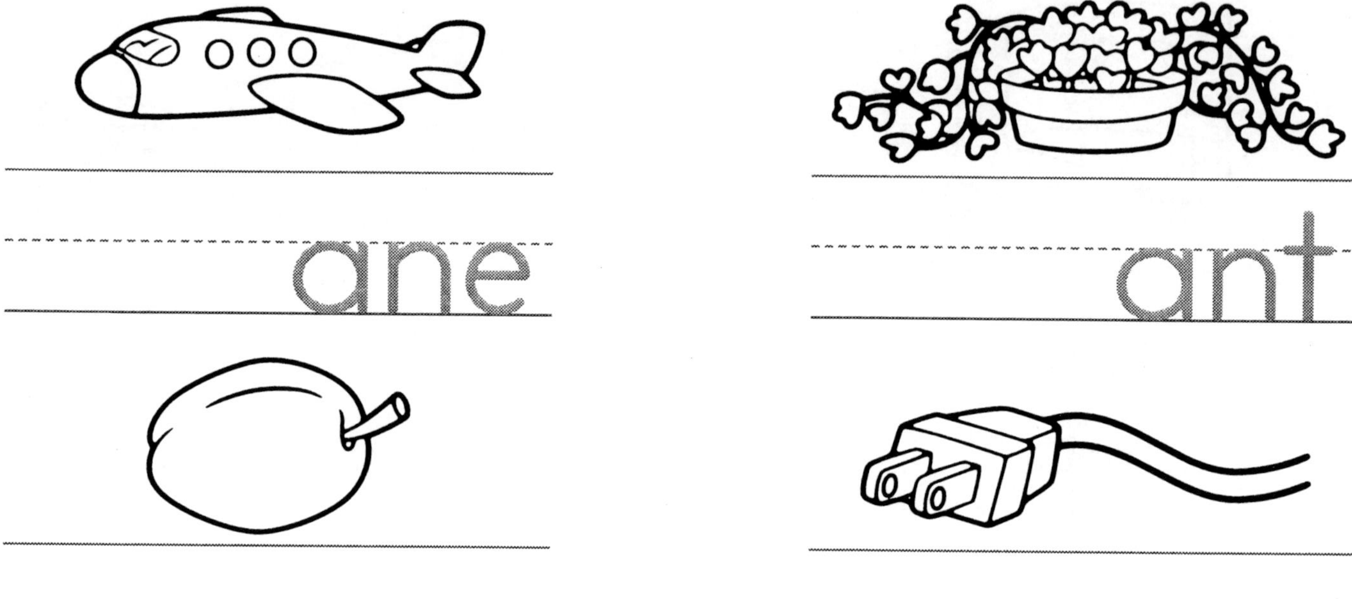

sl

Directions: Listen to the beginning sounds of each item. Circle the items that begin with the **sl blend**. Cross out the other items. Name the **sl blend** items.

Name: ____

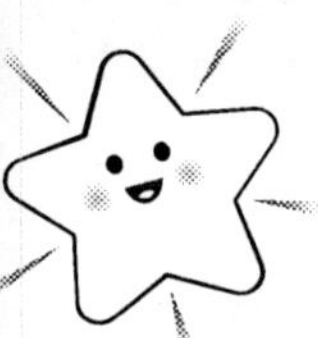

L Blends Review

Directions: Listen to the **beginning sounds** for each item. Write the correct blend to complete each word. Trace and read the words.

bl cl fl gl pl sl

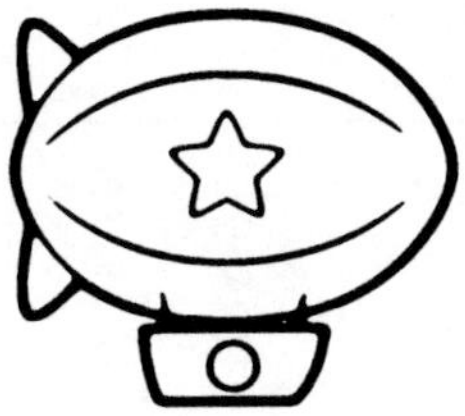

_____imp

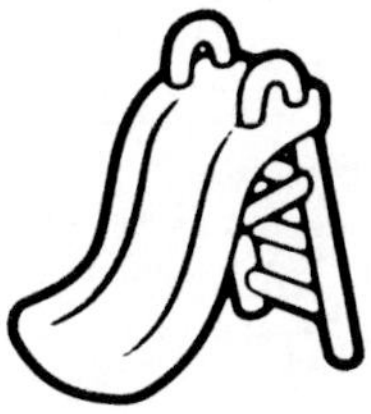

_____ide

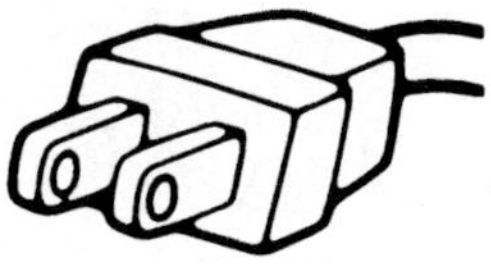

_____ug

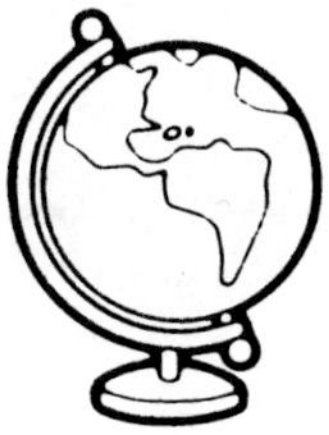

_____obe

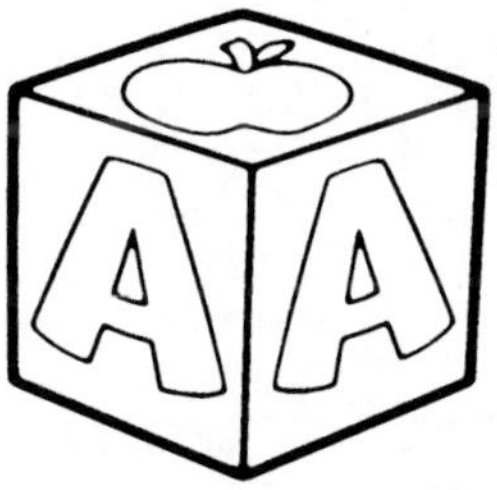

_____ock

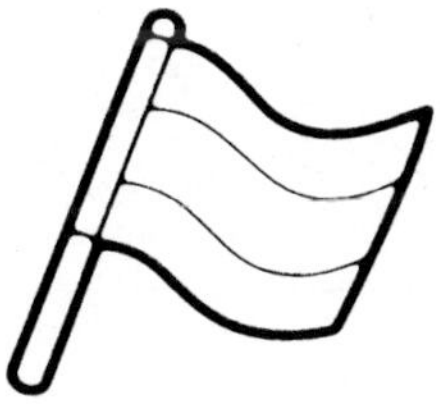

_____ag

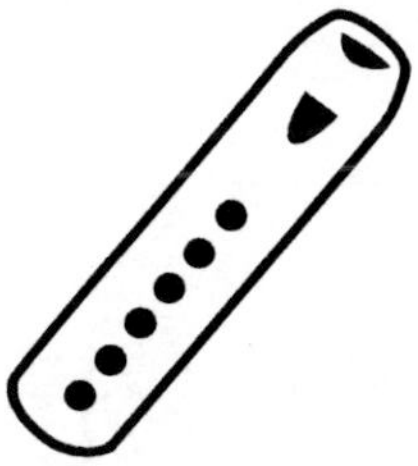

_____ute

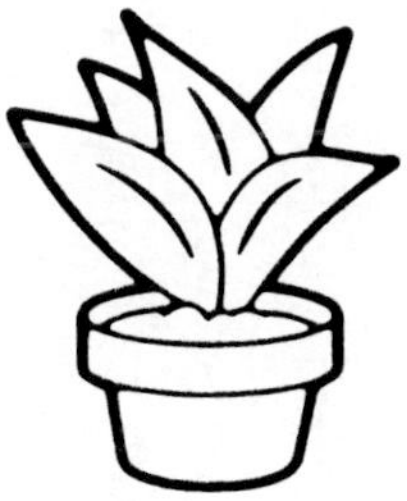

_____ant

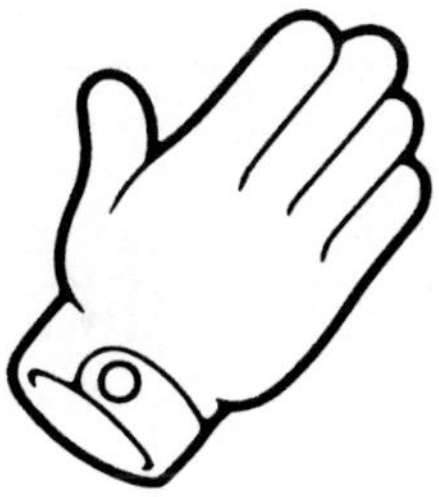

_____ove

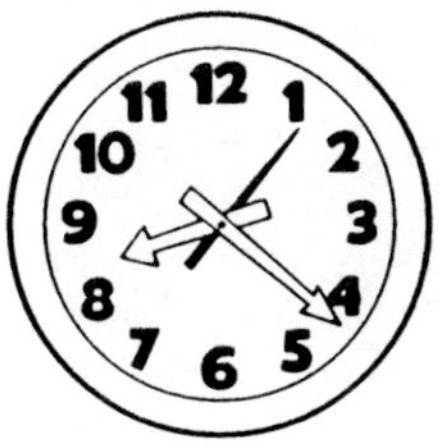

_____ock

Name: _______________________

Choose the R Blend

Directions: Say the name of each item. Fill in the circle for its beginning blend.

  br  cr  dr  fr  gr  tr

  br 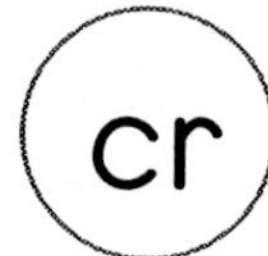 cr  dr  fr  gr  tr

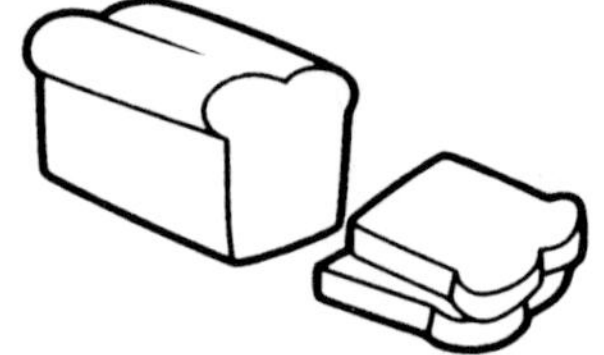  br  cr  dr  fr  gr  tr

  br  cr  dr  fr  gr  tr

  br  cr  dr  fr  gr  tr

  br  cr  dr  fr gr  tr

  br  cr  dr fr gr  tr

Name: _______________________________

Choose the L Blend

Directions: Say the name of each item. Fill in the circle for its beginning blend.

  bl  cl  fl  gl  pl  sl

  bl  cl  fl  gl  pl  sl

  bl 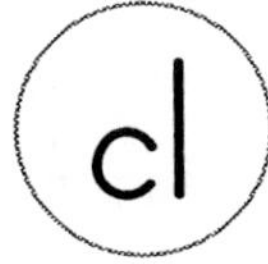 cl  fl  gl  pl  sl

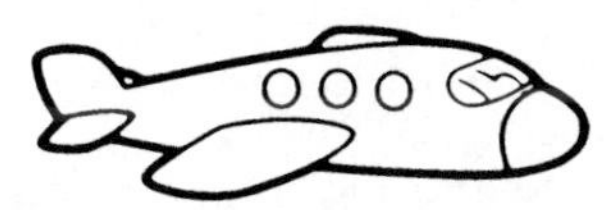  bl  cl  fl  gl  pl  sl

  bl  cl  fl  gl  pl  sl

 bl cl  fl  gl  pl  sl

 bl cl  fl  gl  pl  sl

Answer Key

Page 17
Check that the uppercase and lowercase letters have been filled in correctly.
Circle: Cc, Kk, Oo, Pp, Ss, Vv, Ww, Xx, Zz

Page 18
Circle: bat, bear, bird, ball, bananas, blocks
Cross out: sun, car, train

Page 19
Circle: carrot, car, cow, couch (cross out if called as "sofa"), corn, cat
Cross out: bed, elephant, doll

Page 20
Circle: deer, desk, dominoes, duck, door, dinosaurs
Cross out: bus, bike, hammer

Page 21
Circle: fish, fins, frog, fork, football, flag
Cross out: moon, sun, rabbit (bunny)

Page 22
Row 1: bat, dog, fan
Row 2: cat, drum, can
Row 3: foot, fox, bell

Page 23
Circle: goose, grapes, guitar, gas, gum, grasshopper, gate
Cross out: mouse, drum

Page 24
Circle: house, hose, hand, hat, heart, hive
Cross out: carrot, tree, elephant

Page 25
Circle: jump rope, jar (of jellybeans), jet, jacket, juice, jug
Cross out: fan, web, mittens

Page 26
Circle: keys, kite, king, kangaroo, kittens
Cross out: mop, turtle, pail (bucket), necklace

Page 27
Row 1: hive, jet, gate
Row 2: jar, hose, king
Row 3: gas, kite, hand

Page 28
Circle: leaves, log, ladder, lamp, lion, leg
Cross out: helicopter, pants, cupcake

Page 29
Circle: moon, mailbox, mittens, map, milk, mouse
Cross out: flowers (bouquet), butterfly, pot

Page 30
Circle: nest, net, needle, necklace, numbers, nails
Cross out: watch, rocket, soap

Page 31
Circle: pencil, pie, piano, pizza, popcorn, pumpkin
Cross out: cat (kitten), drum, bunny (rabbit)

Page 32
Row 1: pen, leg, moon
Row 2: mug, pan, net
Row 3: nest, lamp, pot

Page 33
Circle: quail, quarter, queen, question marks, quilt
Cross out: turtle, hose, bow, plane

Page 34
Circle: racoon, rainbow, rake, ram, ring, rabbit, rocket
Cross out: owl, book

Page 35
Circle: sun, saw, soap, star (starfish), socks, six
Cross out: mittens, hammer, hose

Page 36
Circle: turtle, tape, tent, train, tiger, teapot
Cross out: snake, puppy (dog), fish

Page 37
Row 1: quilt, ten, sun
Row 2: rake, ring, sock
Row 3: top, six, quail

Page 38
Circle: van, vacuum, vine, volcano, vest, violin, vase
Cross out: cap (hat), spider/web

Page 39
Circle: window, watermelon, web, well, worm, watch
Cross out: heart (valentine), balloon, keys

Page 40
Circle: yo-yo, yarn, yell, yolk, yak
Cross out: teddy bear, umbrella, frog, plane (jet)

Page 41
Circle: zebra, zero, zigzag, zipper, zoo, zucchini
Cross out: ladder, snowman, dinosaur (stegosaurus)

Page 42
Row 1: zipper, violin, yo-yo
Row 2: watch, wagon, vase
Row 3: zebra, yarn, worm

Page 43
Row 1: Fill in the *f* for fox, the *c* for camel, the *h* for horse.

Row 2: Fill in the *k* for kangaroo, the *w* for walrus, the *m* for monkey.
Row 3: Fill in the *q* for quail, *s* for seahorse, *p* for panda.

Page 44
Row 1: Fill in the *b* for beaver, *g* for gorilla, *n* for narwhal.
Row 2: Fill in the *t* for turkey, *r* for racoon, *z* for zebra.
Row 3: Fill in the *j* for jellyfish, *d* for dolphin, *l* for lion.

Page 45
Row 1: Fill in the *b* for buttons, *m* for mouse, *q* for queen.
Row 2: Fill in the *n* for nest, *p* for pumpkin, *d* for dog.
Row 3: Fill in the *p* for pig, *j* for jet, *s* for sun.

Page 46
Circle: web, crib, tub
Cross out: bat
Add a *b*: sub, cub, bib
Underline: Bob, sub, tub

Page 47
Circle: bed, cloud, bread, bird
Cross out: dog (puppy), doll
Draw faces: Discuss words and faces drawn to check that reader understands words.

Page 48
Circle: leg, mug, jug, rug
Cross out: truck
Words that end in *g*: pig, log, wig, dog; pig and wig rhyme
dog and log rhyme
Underline: big, bug, log

Page 49
Circle: mail, heel, sail, seal
Cross out: door
Underline: small, girl, will, hill

Page 50
Row 1: mug, bed, crib
Row 2: cub, jug, seal
Row 3: web, dog, bird

Page 51
Add an *m*: gum, ham, jam, ram
Underline: ram, him

Page 52
Circle: van, bun, fan, sun
Cross out: drum, net
Add an *n*: pan, pin, pen—The words have different vowels but the same beginning and ending letters.
Underline: hen, barn

Answer Key (cont.)

Page 53
Circle: mop, top, cup, map
Cross out: can, pot
Underline: pup, cup

Page 54
Circle: car, deer, door, pear, four
Cross out: robot
Clap: 2 times for two syllables in the word "feather"
Underline: star, door

Page 55
Row 1: cup, car, fan
Row 2: ram, mop, jar
Row 3: sun, gum, top

Page 56
Circle: bus, dress, gas, grass
Cross out: ship (boat), cow

Page 57
Add a *t*: hat, net, bat, jet, cot
Clap: 2 times for two syllables in the word "carrot"

Page 58
Circle: bow, cow, saw
Cross out: cot
Add a *w*: bow, arrow, rainbow, window

Page 59
Circle: ax, fox, box, six
Cross out: x-ray, wagon
Number of syllables: 6

Page 60
Row 1: ax, bus, jet
Row 2: fox, sax, rat
Row 3: bat, six, gas

Page 61
Row 1: Fill in the *b* for web, fill in the *r* for car, fill in the *p* for mop.
Row 2: Fill in the *n* for can or the *p* for the soup, fill in the *d* for bed, fill in the *g* for pig.
Row 3: Fill in the *x* for box, fill in the *l* for seal, fill in the *m* for gum.

Page 62
g: Circle the *gift bag* and the *pig*. Cross out the *gum*.
x: Circle the *sax* and the *fox*. Cross out the *jet*.
r: Circle the *pear* and the *door*. Cross out the *box*.
b: Circle the *tub* and the *sub*. Cross out the *bunny*.
t: Circle the *robot* and the *pot*. Cross out the *cloud*.
s: Circle the *grass* and the *bus*. Cross out the *sun*.

Page 63
Add an *a*: fan, ham, cap, cat, van, mat
Apple has 2 syllables and *banana* has 3 syllables.

Page 64
Add an *e*: bed, jet, men, hen, leg, web
Elephant has 3 syllables and *elf* has 1 syllable.

Page 65
Add an *i*: bib, pig, pin, fin, six, dip
Kitten has 2 syllables and *mixer* has 2 syllables.

Page 66
Add an *o*: dog, top, pot, mop, box, mom
Otter has 2 syllables and *octopus* has 3 syllables.

Page 67
Add a *u*: bug, tub, nut, cup, cub, sun
Umpire has 2 syllables and *umbrella* has 3 syllables.

Page 68
Fill in the *a* for *bat*.
Fill in the *u* for *tub*.
Fill in the *i* for *pig*.
Fill in the *u* for *cup*.
Fill in the *a* for *ax*.
Fill in the *o* for *pot*.
Fill in the *e* for *jet*.

Page 69
Cross out the *web* in the *a* row.
Cross out the *mop* in the *e* row.
Cross out the *gas* in the *i* row.
Cross out the *bat* in the *o* row.
Cross out the *net* in the *u* row.

Page 70
Rhyming pairs:
bun and *sun*; *bug* and *mug*
fan and *can*; *fox* and *box*
jet and *net*; *pig* and *wig*

Page 71
Rhyming pairs:
a—*bat* and *cat*
e—*men* and *pen*
i—*fin* and *pin*
o—*top* and *mop*
u—*mug* and *bug*

Page 72
Word Family *-am*
ham, jam, ram, yam
Word Family *-ap*
cap, lap, map, nap

Page 73
Word Family *-an*
can, fan, man, pan, van
Word Family *-at*
bat, cat, hat, mat, rat

Page 74
Word Family *-en*
hen, men, pen, ten
Word Family *-et*
jet, net, vet, wet
Adding *et*
bet, get, let, met

Page 75
Words for the *-ig* wheel can be in any order: pig, big, dig, fig, jig, wig
Words that end with *-in*: pin, bin, fin, win

Page 76
Words that end with *-ip*: dip (or chip)
hip, lip

Page 77
Words that end with *-og*: dog, hog, jog, log
Words that end with *-ot*: cot, dot, pot, hot
Adding *ot*
got, not, tot

Page 78
-ub words: cub, sub, rub, tub
Words for the *-ug* wheel can be in any order: hug, dug, bug, jug, mug, rug, tug

Page 79
Column 1: ball, call, fall, hall, mall, tall
Column 2: bell, fell, sell, tell, well, yell
Column 3: bill, dill, fill, hill, mill, will

Page 80
Three words in each word family:
big, pig, jig
Frog, jog, log
Dad, sad, mad
Ned, red, bed
Run, sun, fun

Page 81
Story 1—Add a hat to the cat.
Story 2—Add a rug under the mug.

Page 82
Add an *e* to make new words: cane, mane, tape, cube

Page 83
cape—Circle the words *cap* and *cape* in the sentence.
tube—Circle the words *tube* and *tub* in the sentence.
huge—Circle the words *huge* and *hug* in the sentence.

Page 84
Row 1: lake, cane, rake
Row 2: cage, tape, vase
Row 3: gate, race, cake

Answer Key *(cont.)*

Page 85
Row 1: bike, kite, pipe
Row 2: dice, mice, tire
Row 3: fire, nine, vine

Page 86
Row 1: bone, robe, dome
Row 2: rope, nose, cone
Row 3: hose
Sight words: so, go, no

Page 87
Row 1: mule, tune, cube
Row 2: tube, dune, June
Circle *mule* and *cute* in the sentence.

Page 88
Sight words that end in *y: my* and *by*
Row 1: cry, dry, fly
Row 2: fry, shy, sky
Three more words: spy, try, why
Circle the **y** in spy, try, why.

Page 89
Fill in the *i* for *bike.*
Fill in the *u* for *cube.*
Fill in the *o* for *hose.*
Fill in the *a* for *rake.*
Fill in the *o* for *bone.*

Page 90
Row 1: vase, tube, robe
Row 2: cone, pine, kite
Row 3: hive, mule, cage

Page 91
Rhyming pairs:
a—*rake* and *cake*
i—*tie* and *pie*
o—*hose* and *nose*
u—*tube* and *cube*
Rice rhymes with *mice.*
Lime rhymes with *dime.*

Page 92
Row 1: Circle the *fruit* and the *suit* and cross out the *ruler.*
Circle the *bee* and the *tree* and cross out the *feet.*
Row 2: Circle the *goat* and the *boat* and cross out the *hose.*
Circle the *rope* and the *soap* and cross out the *bone.*
Row 3: Circle the *rain* and the *train* and cross out the *rake.*
Circle the *vine* and the *nine* and cross out the *kite.*
Row 4: Circle the *fire* and the *tire* and cross out the *dice.*
Circle the *sail* and the *nail* and cross out the slice of *cake.*

Page 93
Long vowel rhymes:
Sentence 1: Circle *Mice* and *dice.*
Sentence 2: Circle *Bake* and *cake.*
Sentence 3: Circle *tube* and *cube.*

Page 94
Rhyming -ake words: cake, lake, rake
Sentence 1: wake
Sentence 2: bake, cake
Sentence 3: take

Page 95
Word Family -ice
dice, mice, rice
Word Family -ide
hide, ride, side

Page 96
Word Family -ime
dime, lime, time
Word Family -ire
tire, fire, wire

Page 97
Word Family -ole
hole, mole, pole
Word Family -ow
bow, row, tow, mow

Page 98
Rhyming words:
Sentence 1: Circle *mole* and *hole.*
Sentence 2: Circle *like* and *bike.*
Sentence 3: Circle *bow* and *row.*
Sentence 4: Circle *fire* and *tire.*

Page 99
Sentence 1: tow
Sentence 2: cone
Sentence 3: time
Sentence 4: lake
Sentence 5: hide

Page 100
Br Blends
Circle: bridge, bread, broom, broccoli
Cross out: banana, bee
Cr Blends
crib, crown
crab, crow

Page 101
Dr Blends
Circle: dragon, dress, drum, dream
Cross out: dog, doll
Fr Blends
frog, frame
frown, fruit

Page 102
Gr Blends
grape, grill, grin
Check that crayons were colored correctly. Circle the *gr* blend in each color word.
Tr Blends
Circle: train, tree, truck, trunk
Cross out: tape, tire

Page 103
Row 1: frog, broom
Row 2: crown, grapes
Row 3: trike, crib
Row 4: drum, frame
Row 5: crab, grill

Page 104
Bl Blends
black, blow
block, blimp
Cl Blends
Circle: cloud, clam, clock, clown
Cross out: car, cone

Page 105
Fl Blends
flag, flute
flower, fly
Gl Blends
Circle: gloves, glasses, globe, glue
Cross out: goat, ghost

Page 106
Pl Blends
plane, plant
plum, plug
Sl Blends
Circle: sled, slippers, slug, slide
Cross out: shell, sun

Page 107
Row 1: blimp, slide
Row 2: plug, globe
Row 3: block, flag
Row 4: flute, plant
Row 5: glove, clock

Page 108
Fill in the *tr* for *train.*
Fill in the *dr* for *dragon.*
Fill in the *br* for *bread.*
Fill in the *fr* for *frame.*
Fill in the *cr* for *crown.*
Fill in the *gr* for *grill.*
Fill in the *dr* for *drum.*

Page 109
Fill in the *cl* for *clock.*
Fill in the *fl* for *flower.*
Fill in the *sl* for *sled.*
Fill in the *pl* for *plane.*
Fill in the *bl* for *block.*
Fill in the *gl* for *gloves.*
Fill in the *fl* for *flag.*